Rug Hooking
for the first time®

Rug Hooking
for the first time®

Donna Lovelady

Sterling Publishing Co., Inc.
New York
A Sterling/Chapelle Book

CHAPELLE, LTD.

Owner: Jo Packham
Editor: Leslie Farmer
Photography: Kevin Dilley for Hazen Photography
Photo Stylist: Jill Dahlberg
Staff: Areta Bingham, Kass Burchett,
    Ray Cornia, Marilyn Goff, Karla Haberstich,
    Holly Hollingsworth, Susan Jorgensen, Emily Kirk,
    Barbara Milburn, Karmen Quinney, Caroll Shreeve,
    Cindy Stoeckl, Kim Taylor, Sara Toliver, Desirée Wybrow

Kooler Design Studio, Inc.
President: Donna Kooler
Executive Vice President: Linda Gillum
Vice President: Priscilla Timm
Editor in Chief: Judy Swager
Staff: Sara Angle, Lori Grant, Karen Million,
Sandy Orton, Nancy Wong Spindler,
JoLynn Taylor

Library of Congress Cataloging-in-Publication Data

Lovelady, Donna.
    Rug hooking for the first time / Donna Lovelady.
        p. cm.
    Includes index.
    ISBN 0-8069-9387-1
    1. Rugs, Hooked. I. Title.

TT850 .L68 2002
746.7'4--dc21
                                                    2002030856
10 9 8 7 6 5 4 3 2 1

Published by Sterling Publishing Co., Inc.
387 Park Avenue South, New York, NY 10016
©2003 by Donna Lovelady
Distributed in Canada by Sterling Publishing
c/o Canadian Manda Group, One Atlantic Avenue, Suite 105
Toronto, Ontario, Canada M6K 3E7
Distributed in Great Britain by Chrysalis Books
64 Brewery Road, London N7 9NT, England
Distributed in Australia by Capricorn Link (Australia) Pty. Ltd.
P.O. Box 704, Windsor, NSW 2756, Australia
Printed in China
All Rights Reserved

Sterling ISBN 0-8069-9387-1

Due to the limited amount of space available, we must print our patterns at a reduced size in order to give our patrons the maximum number of patterns possible in our publications. We believe the quality and quantity of our patterns will compensate for any inconvenience this may cause.

THANKS

We would like to thank Scott and Julie Dixon who so graciously allowed us to use their personal spaces as settings for the photographs in this book.

WRITE US

If you have questions or comments, please contact:
Chapelle, Ltd., Inc.,
P.O. Box 9252, Ogden, UT 84409
(801) 621-2777 • (801) 621-2788 Fax
e-mail: chapelle@chapelleltd.com
web site: chapelleltd.com

Table of Contents

Section 1:
Rug-hooking Basics—10

Section 2:
Basic Techniques—24

Section 3:
Beyond the Basics—52

Section 4:
The Gallery—100

Introduction

The first known example of rug hooking came from the Bronze Age. There are examples of this work in the Oslo Museum in Norway.

Rug hooking started in the United States around the mid 1800s. Women made rugs for their homes using old clothing, torn in strips and hooked into burlap feed bags. Fabric was hard to come by and nothing was wasted. Women would split the burlap feed bags open flat and draw their designs on the burlap with charcoal from the fire. Many times they would use the label design that was printed on the feed bag and hook it. The designs of early rugs were very primitive. Most of the design themes were taken from familiar objects—houses, trees, pets, flowers, birds, etc.

In the 1860s, a tin peddler named Edward Frost began designing patterns and printing them onto burlap to sell to the housewives. Later, patterns began to appear through mail order in The Montgomery Ward Catalog.

Rug Hooking for the first time® focuses on the "primitive style" of rug hooking. In addition to it, I have listed some other styles that are very popular and widely used, both among creators and buyers of hooked pieces today.

Primitive: These rugs are made with wide strips of cloth, usually ¼" to ½" wide. They are not realistic in style or coloring; they are unsophisticated and simple. Childhood drawings make great patterns for primitive rugs. You can be very original and creative with this charming style of rug.

Realistic: These rugs are hooked with a very narrow strip of wool, ⅔₃" wide. There are many shades of color used when designing with this very challenging style. To achieve a look of realism, only white wool can be used, which is then dyed as needed. A hooked flower or other object is made to look as real as possible.

Pictorial: With this style, the designer creates a picture or a painting such as a landscape or farm scene. Pictorial designs can be hooked using wide cuts of wool, in the primitive style, or using narrow strips of wool for a more realistic look. These rugs usually tell a story.

Geometric: This style is known for an arrangement of squares, circles, triangles, or diamonds hooked individually and repeated over the surface of the rug. These are great rugs for beginners. You may hook this style, using wide cuts of wool or using narrower strips of wool.

Waldoboro: After a Waldoboro design is hooked, the wool is cut and sculpted, creating a three-dimensional design. This rug is named after the town of Waldoboro, Maine, where the style originated. It is usually used as a wall hanging, as the sculpted wool is difficult to walk on.

How difficult is rug hooking?

Rug hooking is one of the easiest crafts to learn and the most forgiving. There is really only one stitch to learn. After you have mastered that stitch you can hook anything!

Is it expensive to hook?

Just as in any other hobby that you take up, there is an expense involved in rug hooking. You can spend as much or as little as you want. There are different prices and categories to the equipment and materials.

Hooking with "new" wool can become expensive. I hook with mostly "recycled" wool—clothing from the Salvation Army and thrift stores or wool clothing that friends have given me.

How to use this book

For the first-time rug hooker, this book provides information on choosing supplies, learning rug-hooking techniques, and creating hooked projects.

Section 1, Rug-hooking Basics, provides you with the information you need to select the basic tools necessary for this craft. You will learn how to prepare the wool for cutting and how to transfer a pattern to your backing fabric.

Section 2, Basic Techniques, teaches the basic techniques of hooking. You will learn how to form the loops that make up the pile of your rug. You will also learn how to put your projects together.

Section 3, Beyond the Basics, expands on what you will now already know about hooking. In this section, you will learn how to do those extra things that make your projects special.

Section 4, The Gallery, displays some wonderful ideas and designs by artists and professionals in the field of rug hooking. It is my hope that their work will inspire and excite you about the craft.

Section 1: rug-hooking basics

What do I need to get started?

Backing Fabric

There are several types of backing fabric from which to choose. (See Photo A)

Burlap is widely used for rug hooking. In the old days, burlap feed sacks were used for the backing fabric. Today we have a better burlap, called Scottish burlap, that comes in 48" to 60" widths, suitable for the wide wool strips used in the primitive style of hooking. *Note: Do not hook on regular burlap because it will fall apart over time and use. You want your hooked piece to become an heirloom.*

Another backing fabric is monk's cloth. This is an even-weave natural-colored cotton which is available in widths of 72" or 144". This is a wonderful backing fabric for large rugs or hall runners. I prefer to hook on monk's cloth as it is softer and more pliable than Scottish burlap and does not shed like burlap does. You can hook on this backing fabric with either wide-cut or narrow-cut wool.

Linen is also used as a backing fabric. It is an even-weave white material, and the most expensive of the backing fabrics. Linen also will enable you to hook with both wide and narrow strips of wool.

Refer to Acknowledgments on pages 110–111 for more information on these backing fabrics.

PHOTO A

Hook

In the early days, rug hookers used a bent nail that was driven into a piece of wood for the handle. Today, there are many shapes and sizes of hooks from which to choose.

For the designs in this book, you will need to use a primitive or coarse hook. I use a primitive hook that was created by rug hooker, Nancy Miller.

You should also invest in a burling iron—a metal tweezer-like tool that enables you to pull your wool loops up evenly after you have hooked them into your project. (See Photo B on opposite page)

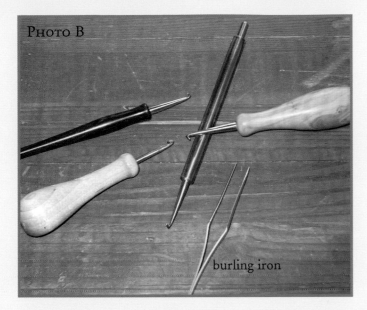

burling iron

Frame

There are many styles of frames available on the market today, ranging from inexpensive to very expensive. The least expensive setup is to use a 14" embroidery hoop and attach it to a tabletop, using a "C" clamp. Because you need both hands to hook, I recommend that you invest in a hoop with a stand, either for the lap or one that sits on the floor. You can get a frame that rotates 360° or one that remains rigid. There are many floor frames in which the hoop has a stand that sits on the floor. Also available is a portable frame that is great for taking your hooking with you when you go somewhere and want to hook.

I have found two types of frames to be the best on the market for hooking. The first is an adjustable hoop frame. The second is a gripper-bar lap frame. The adjustable hoop frame is less expensive, has a hoop for holding your backing fabric, and rotates 360°. The gripper-bar lap frame also rotates 360°, but has gripper bars made up of small metal teeth that make it easier to remove and reposition your project without leaving hoop marks. This frame is more expensive. Whichever you choose, either frame is a good investment, and it is unlikely you will find the need to purchase another. (See Photo C)

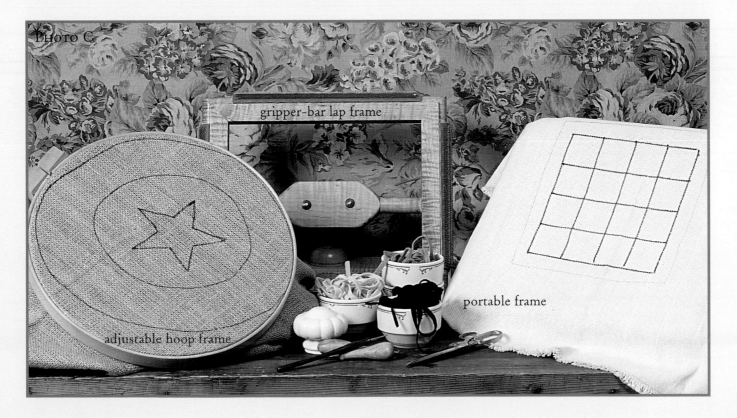

Photo C

gripper-bar lap frame

adjustable hoop frame

portable frame

Scissors

When selecting a pair of scissors for rug hooking, choose offset handled scissors or embroidery scissors. These enable you to get close to the hooking surface while cutting off the ends of the hooking strips. You will also need a pair of shears for cutting the wool and backing fabrics.

Wool

A 100% wool is the best wool for hooking and it takes dyes very well. An 80% wool and 20% other is acceptable if you just love the wool color or pattern. However, sometimes the mixed fabric won't take the dye as well as 100% wool will. Use skirt-weight wool. Coat-weight wool is too heavy to pull through the weave of the backing fabric. (See Photo D)

Photo E

Photo D

Using only new wool can become very expensive. Good skirt-weight wool could cost $30 or more per yard. Get in the habit of prowling the Salvation Army or goodwill stores, thrift stores, and garage sales. By recycling old wool you can keep the cost down and get some wonderful wool in the process. Be certain to put the word out to your friends that their old woolen clothing would be appreciated. (See Photo E)

Look for patterned as well as solid-colored wool. Tweeds, plaids, and textures are also good for hooking. These patterned wools lend a distinct flavor to your designs. Use care though when hooking with patterned wool. Tweeds and many plaids are of a looser weave and can fall apart. Avoid pulling the loops up too hard or the wool will fall apart. Although it takes more care to hook with this type of wool, the effect it creates is well worth the time and effort. *Note: Men's sport coats are a great source for tweeds and plaids.*

Mechanical Wool-strip Cutter

A mechanical wool-strip cutter is a hand-operated cutter. You also can cut your wool with scissors or a rotary cutter that is commonly used for quilting. However, if you are going to do rug hooking as a hobby, you really should invest in a mechanical cutter as it allows you to cut more than one strip at a time. There are several manufacturers of cutters. There are also several different models to choose from. One table model has suction cups for feet that keep it in place on the table. Another cutter model is configured to be mounted on the side of your tabletop. Both models have various sized interchangeable blades that allow you to cut wide or narrow strips. This is another expense for your hobby, but worth the investment. (See Photo F on opposite page)

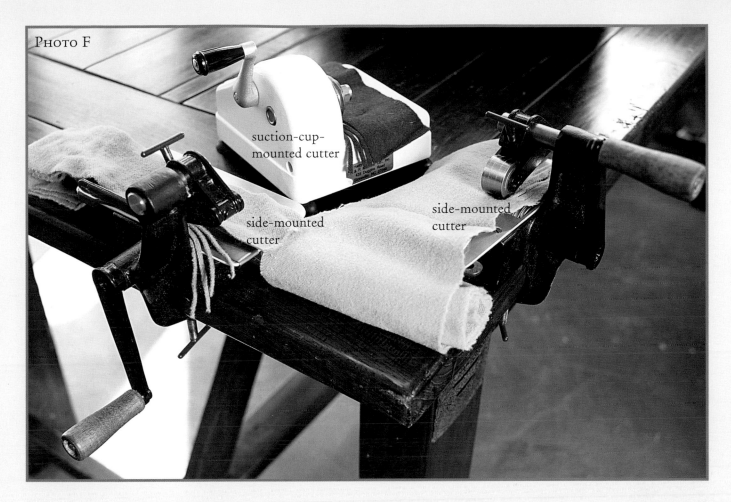

suction-cup-
mounted cutter

side-mounted
cutter

side-mounted
cutter

Other necessary supplies

Clean fluffy towels (dedicated to use for both felting
and tea-dyeing wool)

Iron-on transfer pen for transferring the design
onto the backing fabric

Measuring tools: compass, ruler, tape measure

Needle and coordinating thread for finishing

Pencil for tracing patterns

Permanent marking pen for drawing the design onto
the backing fabric

Sewing machine for stitching a line around the
design to keep the backing fabric from fraying and
for finishing projects

Steam iron and ironing board

Textile dyes for dyeing new wool or overdyeing
old wool

Tracing paper for copying the pattern before transferring it onto the backing fabric

How do I prepare the wool for hooking?

Before using any type of wool, the wool must be
"felted." Felting is shrinking the fibers of the wool.
This process tightens the wool so that when it is cut,
it will not ravel on the edges.

Place new wool in the washing machine, on a hot-
water setting, with a little laundry detergent and
wash for 15 to 20 minutes. Rinse wool in cold water.
It is the hot-to-cold change in the water temperature
that felts the wool. Place the washed wool in the
dryer with a soft towel, which absorbs excess moisture and fluffs up the wool. This process makes your
wool turn thicker, denser, and softer. Your new wool
is ready to cut and strip.

When gathering up old woolen clothing, you must first wash it in the washing machine in warm water with a little laundry detergent. Do not take the clothing apart—wash the entire garment. If you tear the garment apart first, your smaller pieces will become tangled and will be harder to get apart later. Dry the washed clothing in the dryer. After the garment is dry, tear out the linings and remove buttons, zippers, etc. Your recycled wool is now felted and ready to rip apart. *Note: Never take wool that has not been cleaned into your house, as there might be insects in the wool that you do not want in your house. Always wash your wool pieces before introducing them into your wool supply. I keep mine in the garage until they are washed.*

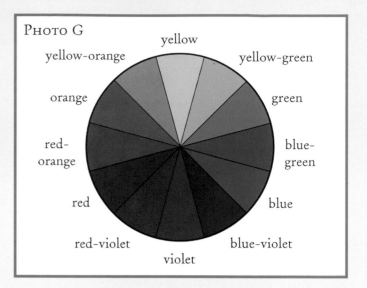

Photo G

How do I know what colors to use?

Think about where you will use your hooked project. What are the colors in that room? You will want to use colors that are compatible to the area where your project is going to be enjoyed. If it is going to be a rug, you should think about how much traffic will be in that area—you may want to avoid using too many light colors that show soil and wear.

A color wheel can be a big help to you when trying to choose colors that go together. Remember that all colors come from the three primary colors: blue, red, and yellow. Hue is the name of a color. Value is the degree of lightness or darkness of a color, and intensity is the brightness or dullness of a hue. Complementary colors are the colors that are directly across the color wheel from each other. You can see this visually with the use of a color wheel. (See Photo G)

When making a primitive-style piece, limit yourself to three or four colors. Too many colors make a design look busy. Primitive pieces are simple. Choose colors that you love to live with.

Be creative with your use of color—cats can be green if you want, leaves can be colors other than green, and flowers need not be the colors that they are in nature. Use your imagination. Make certain that your colors are evenly distributed throughout your design. A good rule of thumb is to make your colors appear in triangles on the design. Spread them out so when they are looked at individually, you could draw a line to the same colors by drawing an imaginary triangle on the design. (See Photo H)

Photo H

If you cannot find wool in the colors that you would like, you can always dye it to meet your particular needs.

How do I dye the wool?

My favorite way to dye fabrics for the primitive style of hooking is to use the "stew-pot method." Try to find a large, white enamel pot at a garage sale or flea market. It's okay if it has rust spots inside. Use this pot only for dyeing your wool—never use it for cooking as the dyes can leave behind toxic residues. A white pot allows you to see the water when it clears. When the water is clear, this means the wool has soaked up all the dye. You will also need a wooden spoon, special dye-measuring spoons, and tongs to pull hot wool out of the pot. (See Photo I)

Before dyeing, prepare your wool by soaking it overnight in your washing machine with a small amount of laundry detergent. This enables the wool to soak up the dye well. Use the spin cycle to remove excess water.

PHOTO I

I recommend getting a book on dye formulas when you purchase your dyes. I use a commercial dye which yields colors that stay nice for years. You may use fabric dyes commonly found in grocery and arts-and-crafts stores, but be aware that the colors will quickly fade in natural light. Information for commercial dyes is found in Acknowledgments on pages 110–111.

Fill the pot two-thirds full of water and bring to a full boil. Add the dye to the pot. Stir the dye with a wooden spoon until all dye is dissolved.

Place wet wool into the pot. If you want the wool to dye evenly, do not put too much wool in the pot. However, to create a "mottling" of the wool, crowd the pot a little. The mottling gives a nice textured look to the wool when you hook it into your project. See the Liberty Crow Pillow on page 75. Notice the lovely variations of blue in the background. Do not worry when some pieces of wool come out darker than other pieces. When you cut the wool to hook into your piece, you will have dark and light mixed together, adding a nice effect.

Boil the wool in the dye solution for approximately 15 minutes, then add ½ cup white vinegar to the boiling mixture. Vinegar is your mordant. This sets the dye in the wool and keeps it permanent. Vinegar, when used as a mordant, makes the colors bright. If you use a noniodized salt as your mordant, your colors will come out duller. This dull look is especially nice in primitive-style rugs as it makes the rug colors look vintage.

Boil wool mixture another 10 minutes. Remove pot from stove and pour contents into sink. Run cold water over the wool until cooled and the excess dye is washed out. Wring out and place in dryer with a soft towel until dry. You are now ready to use your new "designer" colors in your project.

17

How do I cut the wool?

There are several ways to cut wool. One of these is to use a mechanical wool cutter. Another way is to use a rotary cutter that is commonly used for quilt making. If you are using this method, place the wool on a cutting mat and cut the wool. You may also cut wool using scissors. If you use scissors, cut the wool twice as wide as you need and then cut it in half.

Always cut the strips on the straight of the grain or your wool will come apart when you hook it. Tear the wool first into 3"- or 4"-wide strips to obtain a straight grain before running it through a cutter.

Cut wool strips approximately 12" to 14" long. If they are cut any longer, the excess gets in the way. For a primitive cut, you will need to cut your strips ¼" wide. If you are using a mechanical wool cutter, you need to use a #8 blade. (See Photo J) Some designs require that you cut the ¼" strip in half lengthwise. This will give you a narrower strip that measures ⅛" in width. On a mechanical cutter, use a #4 blade. Use this width when hooking faces or tiny details.

How do I know how much wool I will need for a project?

The rule of thumb is to have five times the amount of wool for the space you will be hooking. A 12" strip of wool will hook a 3" line of hooking. It takes approximately 20" of wool to cover a 1" square hooked with loops ¼" high.

PHOTO J

How do I make a pattern to hook?

The first priority is to find or make a pattern that you will love to hook. Primitive patterns are the easiest to create. They are made up of very simple lines without much concern for scale. In the early days of rug hooking, you would see rugs with birds larger than the house, or flowers taller than the house.

In this book, there are 38 patterns for you to use either as instructed per project or as you desire.

Do not be afraid to use your imagination when creating a pattern of your own. Think about where you will place your hooked piece. Begin by drawing your ideas on a piece of paper until you are happy with them. Then make a simple line drawing of the design on a clean piece of paper the size you want your hooked piece to be. Remember, the pattern does not have to be drawn perfectly. The primitive style does not have to be realistic—only the impression of the subject is necessary. So be bold and draw what you love.

How do I transfer the pattern onto the backing fabric?

Measure and cut the backing fabric to the size of your project plus 6" on all sides. Transfer the design onto the backing fabric using one of the following methods.

The first and recommended method is to use a hot dry iron and an iron-on transfer pen. First, enlarge the pattern on a photocopy machine if necessary. Place a sheet of tracing paper on top of your pattern and trace over it using a pencil. Turn the traced design over so it is reading in reverse, then go over the design on the back of the tracing paper using the iron-on transfer pen. (See Photo K) Place the tracing paper on your backing fabric (monk's cloth or burlap) with the right side (pencil side) of your pattern face up. Place a dry hot iron on top of the tracing paper and press down, then move the iron to another area of the paper and repeat. Continue in this manner until the entire design is transferred onto the backing fabric. (See Photo L)

Another way to transfer your design is to use canvas or nylon netting. Place canvas over the pattern and trace over it using a permanent marking pen. Pin the canvas on your backing fabric and trace over the outlines of the design, using the marking pen. The ink will penetrate the holes in the canvas making it come through onto the backing fabric. (See Photo M)

The third method of transferring a design is to use red dot tracing paper, which can be found at your local fabric store. This paper looks like interfacing with red dots that you trace over to transfer the design onto the backing fabric. Follow the manufacturer's instructions for transferring a design using this product.

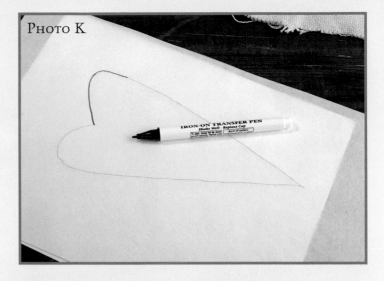

Photo K

Photo L

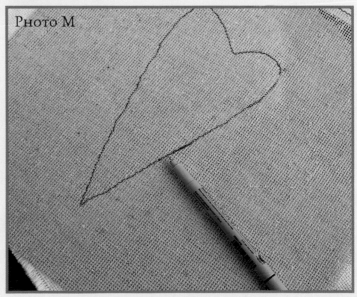

Photo M

How do I prepare the backing fabric for hooking?

After you have transferred your design onto your backing fabric, machine-stitch a line all around the edges of the backing. This will keep the fabric from fraying while you are hooking your design.

Next, machine-stitch a line around the outside of the border of your design. This will keep the hooking from coming out after you cut off the excess backing fabric to finish your rug or pillow. (See Photo N)

Photo O

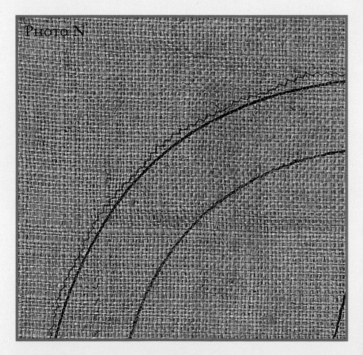

Photo N

Place the backing fabric into a heavy hoop or onto a frame with the design side up. Stretch the backing fabric tightly across the frame. It is very important to keep the fabric tight on the frame while you are hooking the design. Keeping the fabric tight makes it easier to pull the wool through the backing. (See Photo O)

How do I start hooking?

Holding the Hook

Hold the hook in your dominant hand. There are two ways to hold your hook. Some people prefer to hold the hook like a pencil. Others prefer to hold the hook in the palm of their hand with their fingers stretched down the shaft of the hook. (See Photo P)

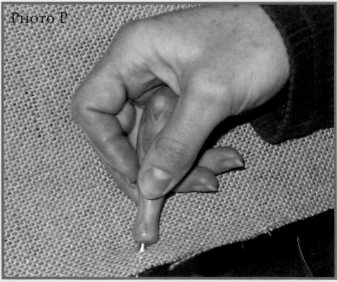

Photo P

Hooking Direction

When hooking a design, you will work sections or portions at a time. Remove the backing fabric from the frame, rotate the backing as needed, replace it in the frame, and begin working the section. If you are right-handed, you will hook your line of hooking from right to left. If you are left-handed you will hook from left to right. Always hook toward you or from top to bottom. It is important to understand that this rule is meant to help you work up the design. It is not to ensure that the lines of hooking run in the same direction across the entire piece. On the contrary, variation in the direction of the lines adds texture and interest. (See Photo Q)

If your design is round, your hooking direction should follow the curve. If it is square, your hooking direction should be vertical or horizontal. Always skip two threads between loops. If you are hooking on the diagonal, you should put a loop in each hole.

Where to Start Hooking

Generally, start in the middle of your design and work outward, hooking the focal point in your design first. Hook a row of stitches to outline the form or shape. Hook just inside the pattern outline, following the contours of the lines. If you hook on the line your design will become larger than the original design was meant to be. When you have it outlined, hook within the area. (See Photo R)

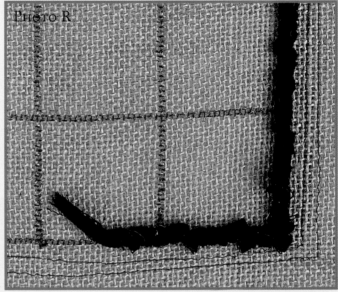

After you have hooked and filled in the central design of your project, remove the project from the frame and replace it with the right corner of the project centered in the frame if you are right-handed or with the left corner of the project centered in the frame if you are left-handed. Now hook a row around the outside borderlines of the design. Remove the project from the frame and replace it until the entire outside borderline is hooked.

The background of the design is usually hooked last. Never start hooking the background first. After hooking design areas, hook one or two rows of background around the hooked design. Hook the background by completing small random shapes until the area is filled.

Remember, start in the center, outline, fill in, then go to the borderlines around the design, and hook the other areas of the design. Hook items that are in the foreground first, then go back and do the background last.

How should the back of my project look?

Turn your project to the back occasionally to make certain that it is smooth and has no loose ends or crossovers. A crossover occurs when the wool strip is dragged across the back of previously hooked stitches to start another spot on your project with out bringing the ends to the front and beginning with a fresh strip. (See Photo S)

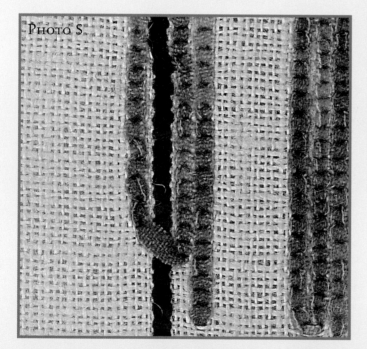

If you have a crossover on the back of your rug, your rug will soon wear out and start to come apart at that point. You should never have a crossover on the back of your rug. If you see any problems, correct them immediately. If you catch your mistakes early, you will save yourself from the chore of ripping out too many loops and becoming discouraged.

When you turn your rug over, you will notice spots where the burlap is showing through, this is okay. However, you do not want to see any of the burlap from the front of your rug. If you do see an opening in the front, go back and fill it in with loops. The back of your rug should look as good as the front. (See Photo T)

How do I steam a hooked design?

Remove the project from the frame and place it, hooked side up, on an ironing board. Wet a towel, ring it out, and place it on top of the project. Place a hot iron on top of wet towel and steam entire project. This steams all of the loops to the same height and hides the trimmed edges of your strips. Your project will look wonderful! Let project lay flat until dry. Your project is now ready to finish. *Note: You may also take your projects to a local dry cleaner and have them steam it with a professional steamer.*

How do I finish my hooked design?

There are many ways to finish a hooked design, limited only by the imagination. A relatively small design can be sewn onto an article of clothing or made into a handbag. Many of the smaller pieces included in this book have been made into pillows. (See Photo U)

Larger designs are usually hooked for the purpose of having a nice rug or wall hanging. There are two traditional ways to finish a rug. You may "whipstitch" the edges of the rug and then apply rug binding tape, or you may finish it with only binding tape. (See Photo V)

If you do not want to whipstitch the edges of your project before putting on the binding tape, that is OK, as long as the piece is not going to get much wear. The purpose of whipstitching the edges of the project is to make the rug more durable. If you are going to place your rug on the wall as a wall hanging, you need not whipstitch the edges. Simply fold the edges to the back of the piece and finish with rug binding tape.

How do I sign and date my work?

You should always sign and date your work. One way to do this is to hook your name and the date into the design of the rug. (See Photo W) You may use a label on the back of the rug. Labels can be purchased at your local fabric store or you can make your own. It is nice to write a bit about your rug or yourself for posterity as your hooked project may last longer than you will.

PHOTO U

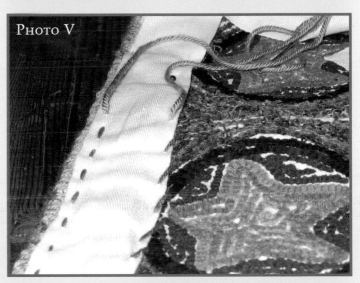

PHOTO V

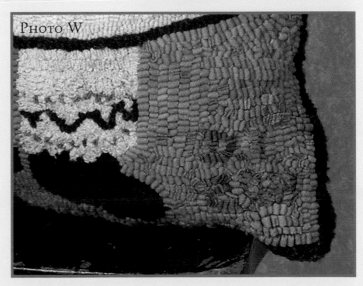

PHOTO W

23

Section 2: basic techniques

1
TECHNIQUE

Materials:
Fabric for pillow back, ½ yd.
Monk's cloth for backing,
    14" square
Polyester stuffing
Wool:
    black for inside border and
        squares, ½ yd.;
    bronze for squares, ½ yd.;
    red for outside border,
        ¼ yd.

Additional Supplies:
Buttons, small (16)

How do I hook
a simple design?

Rug hooking is a craft that you can quickly master. Once you learn the basic technique of creating the stitch, that is about all there is to it—you have taken the first step toward creating something wonderful.

Checkerboard Pillow (See photo on page 25)

The finished size of this pillow is 9" square.

HERE'S HOW:

Preparing the Backing

1. Using ruler and permanent marking pen, center and draw outside borderline, 8" square, directly onto the backing fabric.

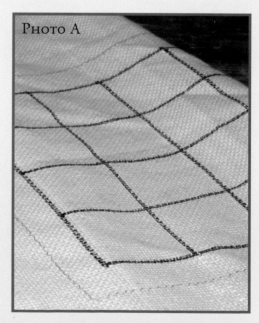

PHOTO A

2. Divide square into 16 equal 2" squares (four across and four down). (See Photo A)

3. Refer to "How do I prepare the backing fabric for hooking?" on page 20. Machine-stitch around outside borderline and position backing fabric in frame. *Note: On this design you can begin in the*

26

This design can be easily enlarged or reduced. Simply add rows of checkerboard onto one or both sides of the pillow. You can also enlarge the size of the checkerboard squares—by hooking a 4" square instead of a 2" square your pillow will be twice as large as the original. Apply this formula to create a matching rug, too.

upper left-hand square of the design since it is all squares.

Beginning to Hook

4. Refer to "How do I cut the wool?" on page 18. Cut wool into strips.

5. Refer to "How do I start hooking?" on pages 20–21. Start in right corner of square if left-handed or left corner of square if right-handed. Holding hook in dominant hand, push hook through backing, from front to back, to its neck. *Note: Your other hand will be waiting underneath the frame, holding the wool strip between your thumb and forefinger with approximately 1" sticking up. This hand is called your "guide hand" and always stays on the underside of the backing just barely touching it.* (See Photo B)

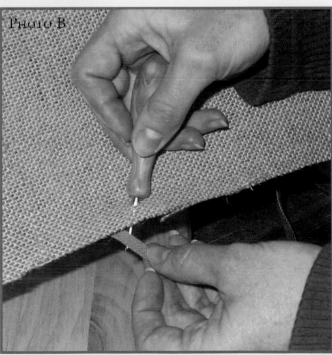

PHOTO B

6. Find hook with guide hand. Feed wool strip onto hook and pull hook and wool up through backing so one end of strip is sticking out on front of backing. Pull wool back with guide hand to leave a tail approximately 1½" long on front. (See Photo C)

Photo C

7. Skip two threads of backing, push hook down through backing, and catch wool strip. Pull wool up to front of backing, forming a loop approximately ¼" high. (See Photo D) Continue hook-

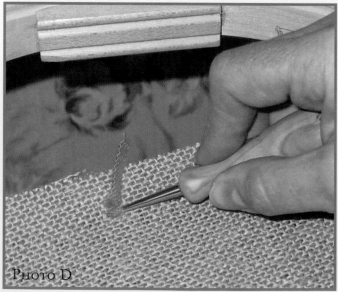

Photo D

28

ing to end of wool strip. *Note: Avoid twisting the wool while hooking. To prevent loops from pulling out, pull loop to the side slightly, a bit higher than the previous loop. When you hook the next loop, it will pull the last one down in height and even with the other loops. When you make a new loop, the previous hole tightens from the pressure of the new loop. It is the pressure of the loops against each other that holds them in place. Do not worry about getting your loops exactly the same height. If they are a little uneven, it's okay. The unevenness will give your rug more character and texture!*

8. Pull remaining end of wool strip to front of backing. (See Photo E) Trim the end to the same height as the loops, using your offset handled scissors or embroidery scissors. *Note: Always bring the ends of your wool strips to the front of your work. You should never have any strips ending on the back side of your project.*

Photo E

9. Begin new wool strip by hooking its end through same hole wherein last strip ended. *Note: This technique ensures that the same thickness will be in each hole.* (See Photo F on opposite page)

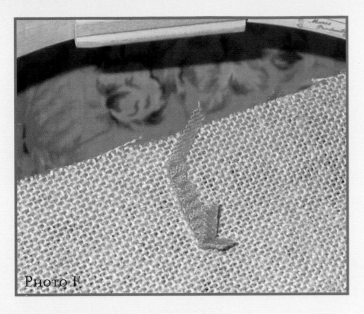

PHOTO F

10. Repeat Steps 7–9 to end of row.

Turning a Corner

11. Turn frame so next row is horizontal and facing you. *Note: Turn the frame so that the direction you are hooking is in front of you. Turning your frame is the key to hooking sharp corners or a pointed end.*

12. Skip two threads between rows and start new row of hooking. *Note: This prevents the hooking from being too tight.* (See Photo G)

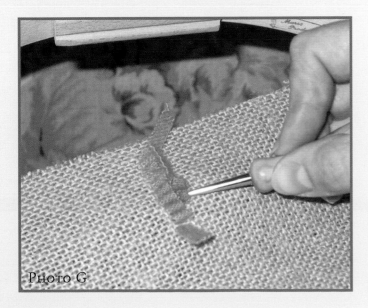

PHOTO G

13. Repeat Steps 7–12 to complete square.

14. Repeat Steps 5–13 to hook each square, alternating colors of squares. *Note: You might not use the entire length of each strip of wool. If you need to change colors, simply bring the strip to the top, trim, and start with a new color.*

15. Hook black and red borders around design.

Preparing the Hooked Design for Finishing

16. Refer to "How do I steam a hooked design?" on page 22. Remove hooked design from frame, then steam hooked design.

Finishing the Pillow

17. Stitch one button onto the center of each hooked square.

18. Cut fabric for pillow back to 10" square.

19. Place hooked piece and pillow back on work surface, with right sides together and hooked side up. Machine-stitch along outside edge of first row of hooking. Leave a 5" opening at bottom of pillow for turning. *Note: Stitching along the hooked line keeps your backing fabric from showing through when the piece is turned.*

20. Trim excess fabric from edge of pillow. Do not trim inside original machine stitching. This will keep the backing from unraveling and hooking from coming out.

21. Turn pillow right side out, pushing out corners.

22. Stuff pillow and hand-stitch opening closed.

Tip

Make it a habit to check the back of your hooking often. By checking the back, you will be able to find possible mistakes and correct them quickly.

2

TECHNIQUE

WHAT YOU NEED TO GET STARTED

Materials for one chair pad:

Burlap for backing,
   21" square
Rug binding tape, 1½" wide,
   1¼ yds.
Wool:
   black for outside border,
      ¼ yd.;
   burgundy for background,
      ½ yd.;
   gold for inside border and
      star, ¼ yd.
Wool yarn, black, 1 skein

Additional Supplies:

#13 tapestry needle

How do I hook a point and finish a round shape?

Visual interest is very important in the design of rug-hooking projects. This star with sharp points set in a perfectly round circle immediately attracts attention. The contrast of the shapes is accentuated by the use of contrasting colors of wool.

Star Chair Pad

The finished size of this chair pad is 13½" diameter.

HERE'S HOW:

Preparing the Backing

1. Refer to "How do I transfer the pattern onto the backing fabric?" on page 19. Transfer Star Chair Pad Pattern on page 32 onto backing fabric.

2. Refer to "How do I prepare the backing fabric for hooking?" on page 20. Machine-stitch around outside borderline and position backing fabric in frame.

Beginning to Hook

3. Refer to "How do I cut the wool?" on page 18. Cut the wool into strips.

Hooking a Point

4. Refer to Technique 1 "How do I hook a simple design?" Steps 5–9 on pages 27–29. Begin in one corner of star. Hook out to a point.

5. Turn frame so the next line is horizontal and facing you.

7. Hook to the next corner of star and turn frame again.

8. Hook out to the next point.

9. Repeat Steps 5–8 until entire star is outlined.

Hooking Shapes and Background

10. Hook inner area of star.

11. Hook borders of design.

12. Hook background area in small random forms until it is filled. *Note: Hooking the background with small random shapes fills in the area faster and is less boring than doing one row at a time around the central design.* (See Photo B)

6. Skip two threads and hook another loop. *Note: This loop will sit right beside the second to last loop in the first line.* (See Photo A)

Photo A

Photo B

31

Preparing the Hooked Design for Finishing

13. Refer to "How do I steam a hooked design?" on page 22. Remove hooked design from frame, then steam the hooked design.

Finishing the Edges

14. Thread tapestry needle with two strands of yarn. Make a running stitch around the edge of the design in backing fabric as close to the hooking as possible. (See Photo C)

15. Gently pull yarn ends to slightly gather backing fabric.

16. Turn excess backing fabric ¼" from hooking to back of design, then, using steam iron, press so edges lay flat.

17. Position needle under folded backing, insert needle into backing close to hooking, and pull through from back to front of design. Wrap or "whip" yarn over folded edge of backing. Insert needle into backing fabric next to previous stitch and pull from back to front again. Continue in this manner, whipstitching all around design to finish edges.

18. Trim excess backing fabric to 1" from whipstitching. Using hand-sewing needle and thread, stitch trimmed backing fabric to back of design.

19. Place rug binding tape at edge of whipstitching, covering trimmed backing fabric and tack in place. Whipstitch rug binding tape onto back of the hooked design.

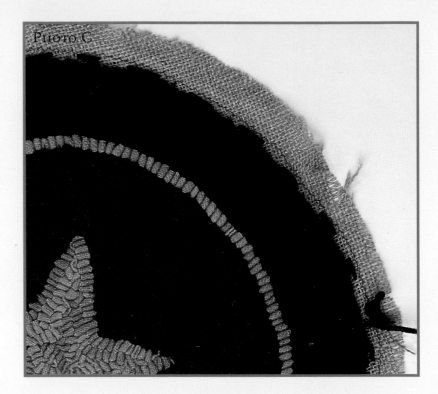

PHOTO C

STAR CHAIR PAD PATTERN   ENLARGE 340%

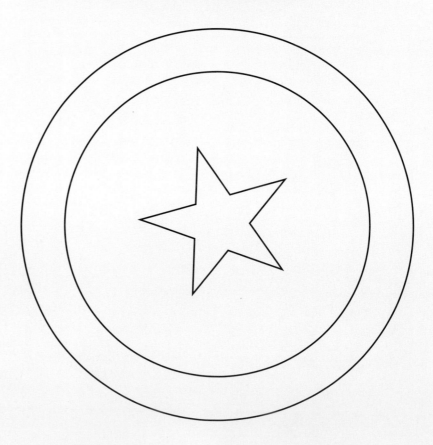

How do I combine shapes and patterns?

Place one shape within another and then set them against a patterned background. The thoughtful combination of three very simple elements—a star, a heart, and a square—results in a dimensional textured piece.

WHAT YOU NEED
TO GET STARTED

Materials:
Fabric for pillow back, ⅓ yd.
Monk's cloth for backing,
   14" x 16"
Polyester stuffing
Wool:
   black for squares, ¼ yd.;
   bronze for squares, ¼ yd.;
   gold for star, 4" x 12";
   red for heart, ¼ yd.

Additional Supplies:
Button, ½" (1)

Checkerboard Heart Pillow

(See photo on page 25)

The finished size of this pillow is 8" x 10".

HERE'S HOW:

Preparing the Backing

1. Refer to "How do I transfer the pattern onto the backing fabric?" on page 19. Transfer Checkerboard Heart Pattern at lower right onto the backing fabric.

2. Refer to "How do I prepare the backing fabric for hooking?" on page 20. Machine-stitch around outside borderline and position backing fabric in frame.

Beginning to Hook

3. Refer to "How do I cut the wool?" on page 18. Cut wool into strips.

Hooking Shapes and Background

4. Refer to Technique 1 "How do I hook a simple design?" Steps 5–9 on pages 27–29. Hook outline of heart.

5. Refer to Technique 2 "How do I hook a point and finish a round shape?" Steps 4–10 on pages 30–31. Hook outline of star, then hook inner area.

6. Hook inner area of heart in small random shapes.

7. Hook borderline of pillow.

8. Refer to Technique 1 "How do I hook a simple design?" Steps 5–14 on pages 27–29. Hook the checkerboard background.

Preparing the Hooked Design for Finishing

9. Refer to "How do I steam a hooked design?" on page 22. Remove hooked design from frame, then steam hooked design.

Finishing the Pillow

10. Stitch button onto center of star.

11. Cut fabric for pillow back to 9" x 11".

12. Refer to Technique 1 "How do I hook a simple design?" Steps 19–22 on page 29. Finish the pillow.

CHECKERBOARD HEART PATTERN   ENLARGE 200%

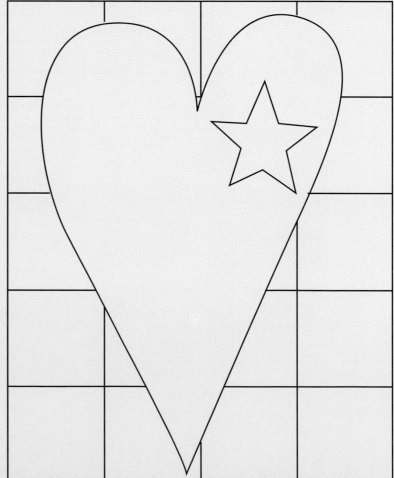

How do I hook letters?

How you make your lettering is a matter of personal preference. Make it the way that you like. You may use both uppercase and lowercase letters when composing your wording or you may choose to use all uppercase or all lowercase letters. You may use block lettering or you may simply want to use your own handwriting.

ABC Pillows (See photo on page 24)

The finished size of the lowercase pillow is 11" x 8".
The finished size of the uppercase pillow is 14" x 8".
The finished size of the stars pillow is 20" x 8".

HERE'S HOW:

Preparing the Backing

1. Refer to "How do I transfer the pattern onto the backing fabric?" on page 19. Transfer Lowercase ABC, Uppercase ABC, or Stars ABC Pattern on pages 38–39 onto backing fabric.

2. Refer to "How do I prepare the backing fabric for hooking?" on page 20. Machine-stitch around outside borderline and position backing fabric in frame.

Beginning to Hook

3. Refer to "How do I cut the wool?" on page 18. Cut the wool into strips.

WHAT YOU NEED TO GET STARTED

Materials for each pillow:
Fabric for pillow back, ½ yd.
Monk's cloth for backing, ¼ yd.
Polyester stuffing
Wool:
   black for background or border and lettering, ½ yd.;
   gold for stars, ¼ yd.;
   red for background, ⅔ yd.;
   white for background or border and lettering, ½ yd.

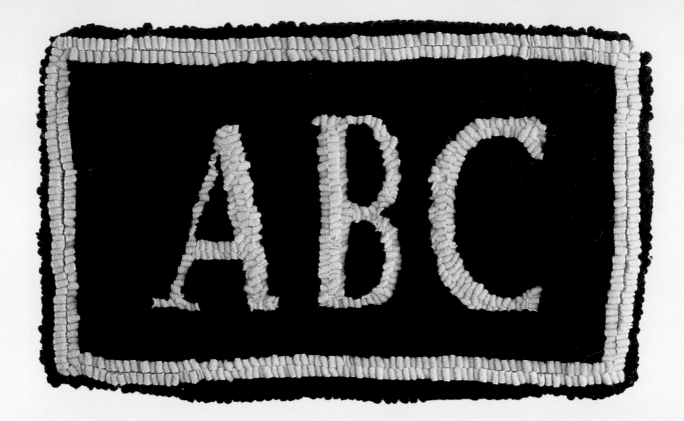

4. Refer to Technique 1 "How do I hook a simple design?" Steps 5–9 on pages 27–29. Hook outline of letters. *Note: You may want to us a darker color for the outline so that the letters will "pop out" when you hook the background.*

5. After hooking outlines, hook inner area of letters, following contours of letters.

6. For stars pillow, refer to Technique 2 "How do I hook a point and finish a round shape?" Steps 4–10 on pages 30–31. Hook outline of the star, then hook the inner area.

7. For uppercase and lowercase pillows, hook inside border with two rows of lettering color, 1" from outside borderline. Hook two rows with background color around inside border. For stars pillow, hook border with lettering color ½" from outside borderline. Hook another row around the border.

8. Begin background by hooking around and between letters. Continue hooking background area in small random forms until it is filled. (See Photo A)

Photo A

36

Preparing the Hooked Design for Finishing

9. Refer to "How do I steam a hooked design?" on page 22. Remove hooked design from frame, then steam hooked design.

Finishing the Pillow

10. Cut fabric for pillow back to 12" x 9" for lower-case pillow, 15" x 9" for uppercase pillow, or 21" x 9" for stars pillow.

11. Refer to Technique 1 "How do I hook a simple design?" Steps 19–22 on page 29. Finish the pillow.

Tips

To create your own lettering, choose a style you like. Some sources for lettering are magazines, newspapers, and computer fonts. Enlarge lettering to desired size on a photocopy machine. Using craft scissors, cut out each letter.

Using a ruler and pencil, draw a horizontal line on a piece of tracing paper. Position the letters on top of the line so that they will be straight. Allow space between letters for at least two rows of hooking. Trace your phrase onto the tracing paper. When transferring the design to the backing fabric, leave at least two rows of stitching between each letter. *Note: If you are doing more than one line of lettering, remember to leave at least two rows of hooking between the lines. If they are hooked too close together, they will look crowded.*

When you are designing your own patterns for rug hooking, take advantage of the knowledge and experience of seasoned rug hookers. There is a wonderful book about lettering by Pris Buttler. Check with your local bookstore for availability. The other book that I would recommend is *Creative Rug Hooking* by Anne D. Mather, published by Sterling Publishing Co., Inc. This book has a large chapter devoted to hooking lettering.

This design idea is great for creating unique monograms. Try hooking a loved one's initials with a mixture of uppercase and lowercase letters. Use that person's favorite colors. If you like, use more than one color and do not be afraid to hook more than three letters as shown here.

Lowercase ABC Pattern   Enlarge 165%

UPPERCASE ABC PATTERN
ENLARGE 225%

STARS ABC PATTERN
ENLARGE 300%

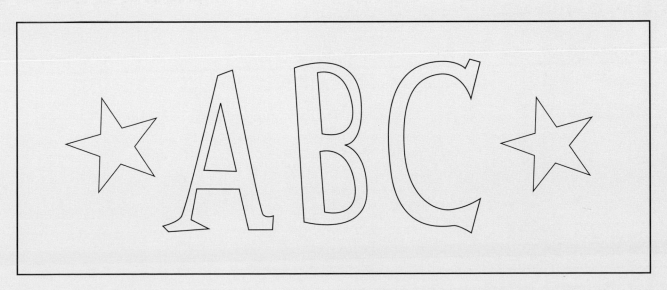

TECHNIQUE

Materials:
Monk's cloth for backing,
   20" x 28"
Rug binding tape, 1½" wide,
   2 yds.
Wool:
   dark khaki green for back-
      ground around stars,
      ¼ yd.;
   gold for border and stars,
      ½ yd.;
   green plaid for background,
      1 yd.;
   red for circles, ¼ yd.
Wool yarn, gold, 1 skein

Additional Supplies:
#13 tapestry needle

How do I hook a border and finish a rug?

This small rug is made up of repeating motifs enclosed by a border, a design that is wonderfully versatile when it comes to extending its size. Simply add on motifs to make a larger rug or hall runner.

Circle and Star Rug

The finished size of the rug is 22" x 14".

Here's how:

Preparing the Backing

1. Using ruler and permanent marking pen, center and draw outside borderlines, 22" x 14", directly onto backing fabric.

2. Refer to "How do I transfer the pattern onto the backing fabric?" on page 19. Transfer Circle and Star Pattern on page 42 onto backing fabric six times, two rows of three.

3. Refer to "How do I prepare the backing fabric for hooking?" on page 20. Machine-stitch around outside borderline and position backing fabric in frame.

Hooking the Rug

4. Refer to "How do I cut the wool?" on page 18. Cut the wool into strips.

5. Refer to Technique 2 "How do I hook a point and finish a round shape?" Steps 4–10 on pages 30–31. Beginning with the middle pair of stars, hook star, then the circle. Fill in around edges of star last.

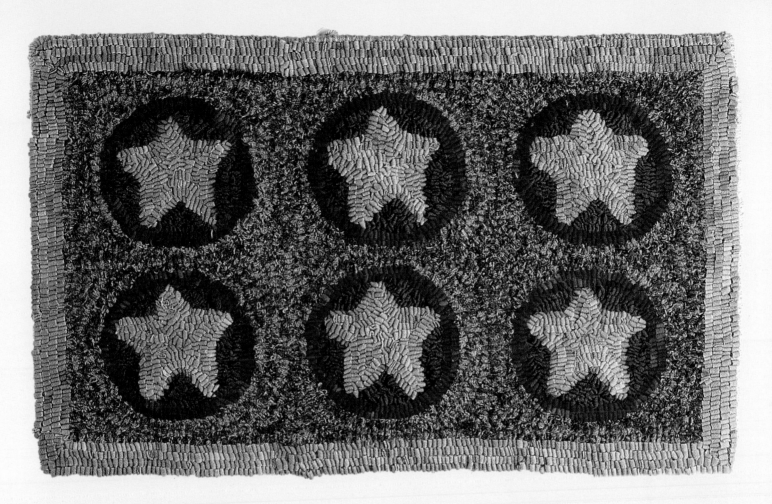

6. Repeat Step 5 for left pair of stars, then for right pair of stars.

7. Remove project from frame, then replace on frame with left corner of project centered in frame. Begin hooking border, starting 1" in from outside borderline. Continue in this manner, removing project and replacing it on frame until entire inner borderline is hooked. *Note: Remember to hook the borderline before hooking the background. This borderline gives you a straight line to hook within.*

8. Continue hooking border by hooking three rows around inner borderline. To ensure a stable edge, hook the last two rows straight around edge of the design. To ensure strong corners that will wear well, hook in every hole starting 3–4 stitches from edge of each corner on the outside row.

9. Hook background area in small random forms until it is filled. *Note: Remember that tweeds and plaids fall apart easier than regular wool, so hook carefully. Avoid pulling too hard or you will pull your strips apart.*

Preparing the Hooked Design for Finishing

10. Refer to "How do I steam a hooked design?" on page 22. Remove hooked design from frame, then steam hooked design.

Finishing the Rug

11. Thread tapestry needle with two strands of yarn.
Fold excess backing fabric ¼" from hooking to
back of rug, then, using steam iron, steam in
place. Position needle under folded backing,
insert needle into backing close to hooking,
and pull through from back to front. Wrap or
"whip" yarn over folded edge of backing.
Position needle under folded backing as before,
insert needle into backing fabric next to previous
stitch, and pull from back to the front again.
Whipstitch all around rug to finish edges. (See
Photo A)

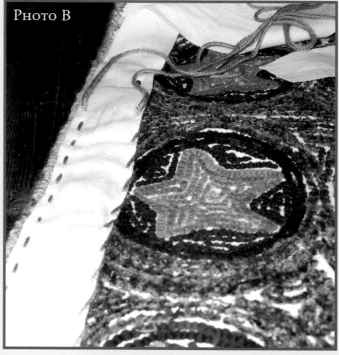

PHOTO B

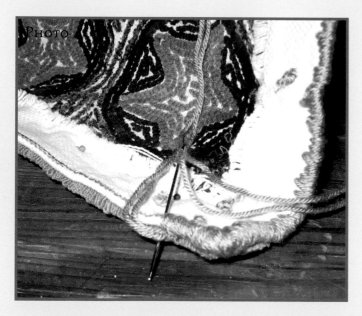

PHOTO A

CIRCLE AND STAR PATTERN
ENLARGE 145%

12. Trim excess backing fabric to 1" from whipstitching.

13. Place rug binding tape at edge of whipstitching,
covering trimmed backing fabric and tack in
place. Whipstitch rug binding tape onto back of
hooked design. (See Photo B)

How do I tea-dye wool?

You can quickly age new wool, using instant tea. Simply dissolve the tea in boiling water and soak the wool in the mixture for a time. The tea-dyed wool gives this rug a vintage look, invoking the spirit of simpler times.

Heart and Hand Rug

The finished size of this rug is 35" x 21".

The rug has been broken down into sections. Reading left to right, section measurements are as follows:

Top of Rug
Large heart section is 6" x 10"
Small heart section is 11" x 4" (hooked with plaid wool)
Checkerboard section (top) is 8" x 3" (squares are 1½"; two rows of four across)
Three stacked hearts section is 3" x 6" (hooked with three different plaid wools)
Small black heart and hand section is 5" x 6"
Hands to work section is 11" x 6" (the lettering is one hooked stitch wide)
Large hand with heart section is 8" x 12½" (the cuff of the hand is hooked with plaid wool)
Heart on side section is 8" x 4"

Bottom of Rug
Checkerboard section is 3" x 9" (squares are 1" x 2"; two rows side by side)
Two black hands with heart in center is 14" x 8" (heart in center is hooked with plaid wool)
Bottom checkerboard section is 8" x 3" (squares are 1½"; two rows of four across)

6

TECHNIQUE

WHAT YOU NEED TO GET STARTED

Materials:
Monk's cloth for backing, 41" x 27"
Rug binding tape, 1½" wide, 4 yds.
Wool:
  black for border, checkerboard, grid lines, and hands, 1 yd.;
  green for lettering and signing your name, ¼ yd.;
  red for hearts, ½ yd.;
  red plaids for cuff and hearts, ½ yd;
  soft red for large hand, ¼ yd.;
  white for background and checkerboard, 3 yds.;
  white for heart in large hand, 10" x 8"
Wool yarn, black, 1 skein

Additional Supplies:
3 oz. jar of instant tea
#13 tapestry needle
White vinegar

Hearts to God section is 8" square (lettering is one
hooked stitch wide)

Inside borders for the sections are one hooked
stitch wide

Outside border of rug is three rows of hooked
stitches all the way around

HERE'S HOW

Tea-dyeing the Wool

1. Tear 3 yd. piece of white wool into strips,
   approximately ¼ yd. wide. Soak wool overnight
   in washing machine with just a little bit of detergent. Use spin cycle to remove excess water.
   *Note: Soaking the wool overnight opens the fibers
   to receive the tea dye.*

2. Dissolve one half of a 3 oz. jar of instant tea in a
   large pot of water. Bring to a boil.

3. Place wet wool in boiling tea mixture. When
   wool reaches desired color, add ½ cup white
   vinegar to pot. Boil another five minutes to set
   color. *Note: If you prefer a darker tea-dyed look,
   add more instant tea to the boiling water.*

4. Remove pot from stove and pour contents into
   sink. Run cold water over wool until rinsed. Dry
   wool in dryer with fluffy towel. *Note: The towel
   helps absorb moisture and remove tea residue from
   the wool.*

Preparing the Backing

5. Using ruler and permanent marking pen, draw
   grid sections directly onto backing fabric, using
   measurements given for "Top of Rug" and
   "Bottom of Rug" on page 43 and at left. *Note:
   If you get confused, refer to the photo for placement of the grid sections.*

6. Refer to "How do I transfer the pattern onto the backing fabric?" on page 19. Transfer Heart and Hand Rug Patterns below and on page 46 onto backing fabric within grid sections.

7. Refer to "How do I prepare the backing fabric for hooking?" on page 20. Machine-stitch around outside borderline and position backing fabric in frame.

Hooking the Rug

8. Refer to "How do I cut the wool?" on page 18. Cut wool into strips.

9. Refer to Technique 1 "How do I hook a simple design?" Steps 5–9 on pages 27–29. Hook black grid lines first. Next, hook design components. Hook background last. *Note: Remember to start in the center of your rug. Start with Large Heart and Hand, then hook one section of the design at a time.*

10. Hook three rows of border around outside edges of design. Start hooking rows from inside border to outside border. *Note: Doing it this way will keep your borderlines even with the design section of the rug. You will be finishing your rug with the outside row of border.*

HEART AND HAND RUG PATTERNS
ENLARGE 155%

Small Black Heart and Hand

Preparing the Hooked Design for Finishing

11. Refer to "How do I steam a hooked design?" on page 22. Remove hooked design from frame, then steam hooked design.

Finishing the Rug

12. Refer to Technique 5 "How do I hook a border and finish a rug?" Steps 11–13 on page 42. Finish edges and back of rug.

Tip

You can change the layout from that which is shown. Use all of the design components or change them around. You may choose to break up this design and do a smaller rug or use some of the design elements individually on pillows. Change the colors to ones you like. The amounts of wool would remain the same; only the colors would be different. Use your imagination and make this design your own.

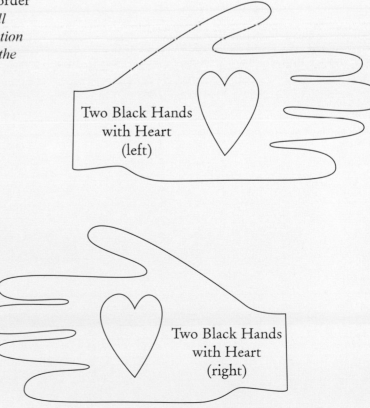

Two Black Hands with Heart (left)

Two Black Hands with Heart (right)

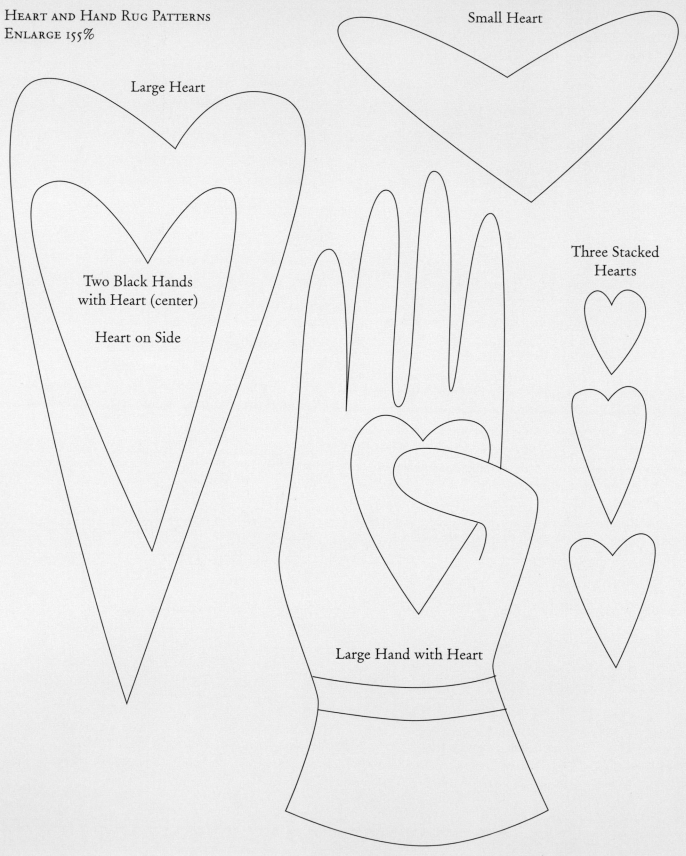

Heart and Hand Rug Patterns
Enlarge 155%

Small Heart

Large Heart

Three Stacked
Hearts

Two Black Hands
with Heart (center)

Heart on Side

Large Hand with Heart

How do I hook lace into my project?

Hook lace into your backing fabric just as you would a strip of wool. Lace is a bit wider than ¼" and, therefore, a bit difficult to pull through to the front, but the effect it creates is worth the effort. The lace gives a hooked piece a nice "popcorn-like" texture.

Heart and Hand Pillow (See photo on page 5)

The finished size of this pillow is 10" x 15".

Here's how:

Tea-dyeing the Lace
1. Refer to Technique 6 "How do I tea-dye wool?" Steps 1–4 on page 44. Cut the recipe for tea-dyeing to one-fourth, then tea-dye the lace, substituting lace for wool in the instructions.

Preparing the Backing
2. Refer to "How do I transfer the pattern onto the backing fabric?" on page 19. Transfer Heart and Hand Rug Patterns—Large Hand with Heart on opposite page onto backing fabric.

3. Refer to "How do I prepare the backing fabric for hooking?" on page 20. Machine-stitch around outside borderline and position backing fabric in frame.

Beginning to Hook
4. Refer to "How do I cut the wool?" on page 18. Cut wool

What you need to get started

Materials:
Cotton lace, 1" wide, 3 yds.
Monk's cloth for backing,
   11" x 21"
Polyester stuffing
Wool:
   gray for background, ½ yd.;
   off-white for hand, ¼ yd;
   red for lettering, ¼ yd.;
   red plaid for cuff and heart,
    ¼ yd.;
   red plaid for pillow back,
    ¾ yd.;
   tan for hand outline,
    8" x 12"

Additional Supplies:
3 oz. jar of instant tea
White vinegar

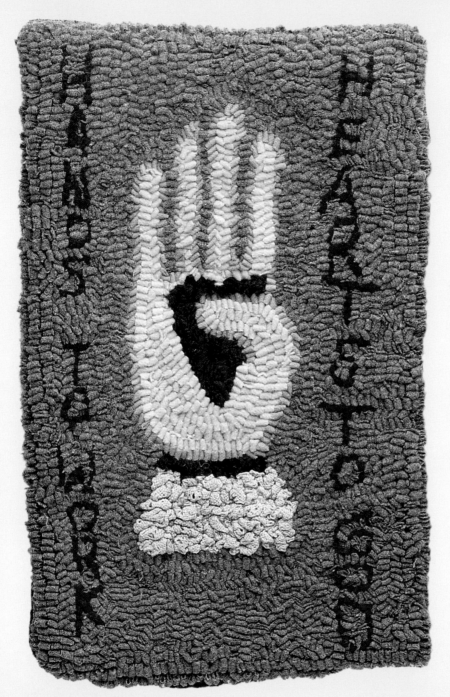

Note: Once a lace loop is pulled to the front, it needs to be spread out a bit, using your hook.

6. Hook borderline of pillow.

7. Hook background area in small random forms until it is filled.

Preparing the Hooked Design for Finishing

8. Refer to "How do I steam a hooked design?" on page 22. Remove hooked design from frame, then steam the hooked design.

Finishing the Pillow

9. Cut red plaid for pillow back to 11" x 16".

10. Refer to Technique 1 "How do I hook a simple design?" Steps 19–22 on page 29. Finish the pillow.

into strips. *Note: Do not cut the red plaid intended for the pillow back.*

5. Refer to Technique 1 "How do I hook a simple design?" Steps 5–9 on pages 27–29. Hook heart outline, inner heart area, hand outline, and inner hand area. Hook red part of cuff. Hook lettering. Hook white part of cuff with tea-dyed lace.

Tip

Be creative when selecting letters and fitting them to a design. The lettering "Hands to Work Hearts to God" is an old Amish saying. I hooked the letters vertically to fit them on the pillow.

How do I hook a face?

Hooking a face is probably one of the most difficult things to do in rug hooking. Since this book is about the primitive style of rug hooking, we do not have to do a lot of details. I cut my ¼" strips in half lengthwise to make the strip narrower. Use this thinner strip to outline the eyes, nose, and mouth; it looks better. Again, do not do a lot of detail, just do enough to give the impression of the facial features.

Rug Doll (See photo on page 51)

The finished size of this doll is 6" x 18".

HERE'S HOW:

Preparing the Backing

1. Refer to "How do I transfer the pattern onto the backing fabric?" on page 19. Transfer Rug Doll Pattern on page 51 onto the backing fabric.

2. Refer to "How do I prepare the backing fabric for hooking?" on page 20. Machine-stitch around outside borderline and position backing fabric in frame.

Beginning to Hook

3. Refer to "How do I cut the wool?" on page 18. Cut wool into strips. Cut flesh, blush, and soft brown wool into ⅛" wide strips. Cut a few black and white strips to this width for the eyes.

WHAT YOU NEED TO GET STARTED

Materials:
Fabric for doll back, ½ yd.
Monk's cloth or burlap for backing, 12" x 22"
Polyester stuffing
Wool:
  black for eyebrows, eyes, and hair, 4" x 10";
  blue for cuffs and dress, ¼ yd.;
  blush for cheeks and mouth, 4" x 10";
  flesh for face and hands, 10" square;
  gold plaid for basket, 4" x 10";
  red for doll body, ¼ yd.;
  soft brown for nose, 2" x 10";
  white for eyeballs and napkin, 1" x 8"

Additional Supplies:
Buttons, ½" (3)

4. Refer to Technique 1 "How do I hook a simple design?" Steps 5–9 on pages 27–29. Outline the face with flesh.

5. Hook outline of hairline with ¼" black strips.

6. Hook eyes with ⅛" black and white strips. Hook the top curve of the eye and just a little bit in the corner. Hook black in the center to simulate the eyeball. *Note: Avoid doing a lot of detail. Simply give the impression of an eye. You can put a little highlight dot in the left corner of each eye to give it a highlight if you want. Do not hook the bottom line of the eye. If you outline the entire eye, the eyes will end up looking very scary.*

7. Hook the nose with soft brown. *Note: Hook just a suggestion of a nose, remember less is better. Do not hook nostrils or the face will look like a pig. When I hook noses for the primitive look I make a "U" shape for the nose and then add a curve on either side at the top.*

8. Hook eyebrows.

9. Hook mouth and cheeks with blush. *Note: By using a light color here, you will keep the face looking more natural, not garish.*

10. Begin background of face by hooking with flesh around the eyes, nose, mouth, and cheeks. Continue hooking background area of face in small random forms until it is filled. *Note: Until the flesh color is completely hooked, the face will look awful. Do not worry, it will come together.*

11. Hook hair. *Note: It is not necessary to hook ears in a primitive face.*

12. When entire face is hooked, cut tops off all loops, using offset scissors. *Note: Just barely cut the tops off so there are all cut ends. This makes the face look more realistic, not bumpy.*

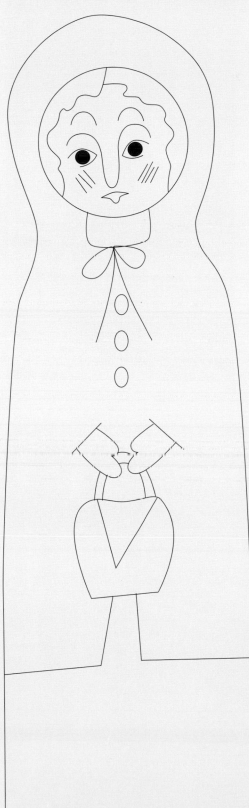

13. Hook remainder of the doll.

Preparing the Hooked Design for Finishing

14. Refer to "How do I steam a hooked design?" on page 22. Remove hooked design from frame, then steam hooked design.

Finishing the Pillow

15. Stitch buttons, evenly spaced, onto center front of doll's body, under face and above hands, as if they are securing the cloak.

16. Cut fabric for doll back to 8" x 20".

17. Refer to Technique 1 "How do I hook a simple design?" Steps 19–22 on page 29. Finish the doll.

18. Tie a strip of red wool in a bow and attach it under doll's chin.

Tip

Take your time when hooking a face. You want it to be just right.

Section 3: beyond the basics

PROJECT

WHAT YOU NEED
TO GET STARTED

Materials:
Fabric for pillow back, ⅓ yd.
Monk's cloth for backing,
  26" x 17"
Polyester stuffing
Wool:
  gold for borders and
    lettering, ½ yd.;
  navy blue for background,
    2 yds.

Additional Supplies:
Buttons, 1" (4)

How do I use a border to make a project larger?

A border is the "frame" around a pillow or rug. Adding a border to your design or expanding an existing one will make your piece larger.

Any size border can be used around a design. You may choose to have a solid border or add lettering around it. You may want to take shapes or motifs from the body of the design and incorporate them into your border area. There are all sorts of border designs from which to choose. By using your imagination when adding on a border, you can make a rug your own design.

Bless Our Home Pillow (See photo on page 56)

The finished size of this pillow is 20" x 11".

HERE'S HOW

Preparing the Backing

1. Using ruler and permanent marking pen, draw outside border-lines of design directly onto backing material. Allow for a 1½" wide inside border.

2. Refer to "How do I transfer the pattern onto the backing fabric?" on page 19. Transfer Bless Our Home Pattern on page 56 onto backing fabric, centered within outside borderline.

3. Refer to "How do I prepare the backing fabric for hooking?" on page 20. Machine-stitch around outside borderline and position backing fabric in frame.

Hooking the Pillow

4. Refer to "How do I cut the wool?" on page 18. Cut wool into strips.

5. Refer to Technique 4 "How do I hook letters?" Steps 4–5 on page 36. Hook "Bless Our Home" with gold.

6. Refer to Technique 5 "How do I hook a border and finish a rug?" Steps 7–8 on page 41. Hook inside border with gold, 1½" in from outside borderline. Add outside border by hooking three rows with navy blue around inside border, then two rows with gold.

7. Hook background area with navy blue in small random forms until it is filled.

Preparing the Hooked Design for Finishing

8. Refer to "How do I steam a hooked design?" on page 22. Remove hooked design from frame, then steam hooked design.

Finishing the Pillow

9. Stitch one button onto each corner of design.

10. Cut fabric for pillow back to 21" x 12".

11. Refer to Technique 1 "How do I hook a simple design?" Steps 19–22 on page 29. Finish the pillow.

Tip

Use a color for the border that appears in the body of the design. It is a good idea to have some rug-hooking books available for reference. They will give you ideas for borders to use on your piece.

How do I make rug hooking wearable?

A relatively small hooked design can be placed on a piece of clothing such as the back of a jacket or, in this case, the bib of an apron. You can use a purchased apron or make one of your own. The appliqué work on this apron is used to accent the pocket.

Heart Apron (See photo on page 59)

The finished size of the large heart design is 11" x 10". Because the hooking and appliqué are made of wool, this project must be dry cleaned.

HERE'S HOW:

Preparing the Backing

1. Using ruler and permanent marking pen, draw outside borderlines, 11" x 10", directly onto backing fabric.

2. Refer to "How do I transfer the pattern onto the backing fabric?" on page 19. Transfer Heart Apron Pattern on page 59 onto backing fabric, centered within outside borderline.

3. Refer to "How do I prepare the backing fabric for hooking?" on page 20. Machine-stitch around outside borderline and position backing fabric in frame.

Hooking the Design

4. Refer to "How do I cut the wool?" on page 18. Cut the wool into strips.

WHAT YOU NEED TO GET STARTED

Materials:
Apron with bib
Monk's cloth for backing,
    17" x 16"
Perle cotton threads:
    blue; gold; red
Wool:
    blue for background area,
        ¼ yd.;
    red for border and heart,
        ½ yd.;
    white for border, ¼ yd.
Wool felts:
    barn red for hearts,
        12" square;
    old gold for stars,
        12" square;
    wheatfields for background,
        12" square

5. Refer to Technique 1 "How do I hook a simple design?" Steps 5–9 on pages 27–29. Hook outline of heart. Hook inner area of heart.

6. Refer to Technique 5 "How do I hook a border and finish a rug?" Steps 7–8 on page 41. Hook inside border with two rows of red, 2" from outside borderline. Hook two rows with white around inside border, then one row with navy blue. Hook two rows with white again, and finally two rows with red.

7. Hook background area with blue in small random forms until it is filled.

Preparing the Hooked Design for Finishing

8. Refer to "How do I steam a hooked design?" on page 22. Remove hooked design from frame, then steam hooked design.

Finishing the Apron

9. Trim excess backing fabric to 1½" from hooking. Fold trimmed backing fabric to back of design, then using a steam iron, steam in place.

10. Using hand-sewing needle and thread, hand-stitch hooked heart design onto apron bib.

11. Transfer Pocket Heart and Pocket Star Patterns below onto wool felt. Cut out motifs.

12. Using a blanket stitch and perle cotton thread, hand-stitch the hearts and stars onto the background felt. (See Diagram A) Accent the points of the star with French knots. (See Diagram B) Using a running stitch, hand-stitch layered motifs onto the apron front or onto pockets. *Note: Layer the motifs as shown on patterns.*

DIAGRAM A

DIAGRAM B

Heart Apron Pattern
Enlarge 155%

Pocket Heart
Pattern
Enlarge 180%

Pocket Star Pattern
Enlarge 180%

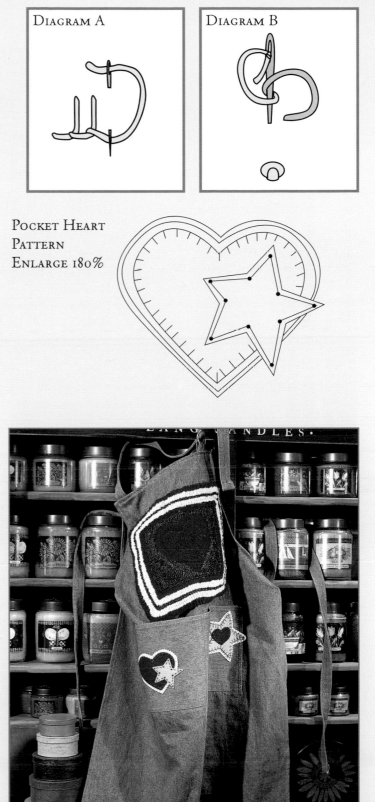

3
PROJECT

WHAT YOU NEED TO GET STARTED

Materials:
Cotton lace, 1" wide, 3 yds.
Monk's cloth for backing, 40" x 33"
Rug binding tape, 1½" wide, 4 yds.
Wool:
  beige for nose area, 2" x 6";
  black for bear outline, clothing, and eyes, ½ yd.;
  blush for cheeks, 2" x 6";
  brown for lettering and teddy bear, ½ yd.;
  plaid for jacket top that goes with pants, ¼ yd.;
  red for border and clothing, 1 yd.;
  tan for background, 2 yds.;
  turquoise for dresses, ½ yd.;
  white for tabs on clothing, ½ yd.
Wool yarn, yellow, 1 skein

Additional Supplies:
#13 tapestry needle

How do I hook polka dots and embellishments?

Add something unexpected to the design of your hooked rug. Polka dots or a thin strip of wool tied into a bow makes a textured piece even more dimensional.

Teddy Bear Rug or Wall Hanging

The finished size of this rug is 34" x 27".

HERE'S HOW:

Preparing the Backing

1. Using ruler and permanent marking pen, center and draw outside borderlines, 34" x 27", directly onto backing fabric.

2. Refer to "How do I transfer the pattern onto the backing fabric?" on page 19. Trace Teddy Bear Hat, Teddy Bear Lettering, Teddy Bear, and Teddy Bear Clothing Patterns on pages 62–64 onto individual pieces of tracing paper for ease in positioning patterns on backing fabric. Transfer patterns onto backing fabric, centering teddy bear within border and arranging hats and clothing around her with lettering at top.

3. Refer to "How do I prepare the backing fabric for hooking?" on page 20. Machine-stitch around outside borderline and position backing fabric in frame.

Hooking the Rug

4. Refer to "How do I cut the wool?" on page 18. Cut the wool into strips.

5. Refer to Technique 1 "How do I hook a simple design?" Steps 5–9 on pages 27–29. Hook outline and inner area of teddy bear.

6. Refer to Technique 4 "How do I hook letters?" Steps 4–5 on page 36. Outline lettering with red. Hook inner areas with brown.

7. Hook outlines for hats and clothing, then hook inner areas.

8. Refer to Technique 7 "How do I hook lace into my project?" Step 5 on page 48. Hook lace into turquoise dress top.

9. Add dots to polka-dot dress by hooking one stitch in and cutting off strip. *Note: It is easier to hook dots after hooking the inner area of the design than to try to hook around them. Do not worry too much about exact polka-dot placement—simply hook them where you can get your hook in.*

10. For bow in teddy bear's hair, push hook through backing fabric and pull up a strip of red wool so end is at front of hooking. Push hook one stitch over, just beside that end, and pull up remaining end of wool. Tie ends in a bow. Trim ends.

11. Refer to Technique 5 "How do I hook a border and finish a rug?" Steps 7–8 on page 41. Begin hooking border of rug 1½" from outside borderline. Hook three additional rows around inner borderline.

12. Hook background area in small random forms until it is filled.

Preparing the Hooked Design for Finishing

13. Refer to "How do I steam a hooked design?" on page 22. Remove hooked design from frame, then steam hooked design.

Finishing the Rug

14. Refer to Technique 5 "How do I hook a border and finish a rug?" Steps 11–13 on page 42. Finish edges and back of rug.

Tips

Feel free to hook these outfits with any colors that you prefer. You can also make the design into a boy bear and draw clothes typically for boys if you like.

You may use this design as a rug or a wall hanging. If you choose to use it as a wall hanging, I suggest sewing buttons down the front of the clothes. I think this would add a nice touch to a wall hanging. However, do not use buttons if you are going to use it as a rug, as the buttons could cause someone to trip and possibly injure themselves.

TEDDY BEAR HAT PATTERNS   ENLARGE 145%

Teddy Bear Pattern   Enlarge 135%
(Enlarge 185% for Teddy Bear Pillow)

Teddy Bear Lettering Pattern   Enlarge 170%
(Enlarge 175% for
"Teddy Bear"
Lettered Pillow)

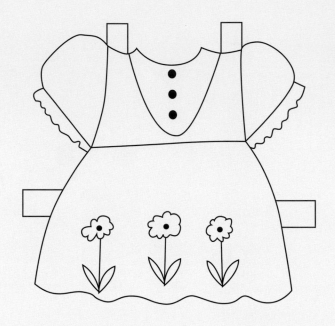

How do I use a motif from another project?

It is easy to create a theme for a room by repeating motifs in different items of decor. This pillow naturally goes with the Teddy Bear Rug or Wall Hanging on page 60.

Teddy Bear Pillow (See photo on page 53)

The finished size of the pillow is 12" x 18".

HERE'S HOW:

Preparing the Backing

1. Using ruler and permanent marking pen, center and draw outside borderlines, 12" x 18", directly onto backing fabric.

2. Refer to "How do I transfer the pattern onto the backing fabric?" on page 19. Transfer Teddy Bear Pattern on page 63 onto backing fabric, centered within outside borderline.

3. Refer to "How do I prepare the backing fabric for hooking?" on page 20. Machine-stitch around outside borderline and position backing fabric in frame.

Hooking the Pillow

4. Refer to "How do I cut the wool?" on page 18. Cut the wool into strips.

5. Refer to Technique 1 "How do I hook a simple design?" Steps 5–9 on pages 27–29. Hook outline of teddy bear. Hook inner area of nose, then hook nose and eyes. Hook cheeks. Hook inner area of teddy bear.

WHAT YOU NEED TO GET STARTED

Materials:
Fabric for pillow back, ½ yd.
Monk's cloth for backing, 18" x 24"
Polyester stuffing
Wool:
  black for bear outline, eyes, and nose, ¼ yd.;
  blush for cheeks, 2" x 6";
  brown for teddy bear, ½ yd.;
  tan for background and nose area, 4" x 12"
  red for bow, 1 strip

Additional Supplies:
Buttons:
  large for pillow corners (4);
  small for bear front (3)

65

6. Refer to Project 3 "How do I hook polka dots and embellishments?" Step 10 on page 62. Hook bow.

7. Hook borderline of pillow.

8. Hook background area in small random forms until it is filled.

Preparing the Hooked Design for Finishing

9. Refer to "How do I steam a hooked design?" on page 22. Remove hooked design from frame, then steam the hooked design.

Finishing the Pillow

10. Stitch three small buttons onto front of teddy bear. Stitch one large button onto each corner of the design.

11. Cut fabric for pillow back to 13" x 19".

12. Refer to Technique 1 "How do I hook a simple design?" Steps 19–22 on page 29. Finish the pillow.

How do I use lettering from another project?

When you find a design you like, it is okay to use bits and pieces of it for different projects. This pillow uses the lettering from the Teddy Bear Rug or Wall Hanging on page 60 and has a new coordinating border.

"Teddy Bear" Lettered Pillow
(See photo on page 53)

The finished size of the pillow is 19" x 10".

HERE'S HOW:

Preparing the Backing

1. Using ruler and permanent marking pen, center and draw outside borderlines, 19" x 10", directly onto backing fabric.

2. Refer to "How do I transfer the pattern onto the backing fabric?" on page 19. Transfer Teddy Bear Lettering Pattern on page 63 onto backing fabric, centered within outside borderline.

3. Refer to "How do I prepare the backing fabric for hooking?" on page 20. Machine-stitch around outside borderline and position backing fabric in frame.

Hooking the Pillow

4. Refer to "How do I cut the wool?" on page 18. Cut the wool into strips.

5. Refer to Technique 4 "How do I hook letters?" Steps 4–5 on page 36. Hook outline of lettering. Hook inner areas.

WHAT YOU NEED TO GET STARTED

Materials:
Fabric for pillow back, ⅓ yd.
Monk's cloth for backing,
    25" x 16"
Polyester stuffing
Wool:
    red for border and lettering,
        ¼ yd.;
    tan for background, ½ yd.;
    turquoise for border, ¼ yd.

6. Refer to Technique 5 "How do I hook a border and finish a rug?" Steps 7–8 on page 41. Hook inside border with one row of turquoise 1¾" from outside borderline. Hook one row with red around inside border, then two rows with turquoise. Finally, hook two rows with red.

7. Hook background area in small random forms until it is filled.

Preparing the Hooked Design for Finishing

8. Refer to "How do I steam a hooked design?" on page 22. Remove hooked design from frame, then steam hooked design.

Finishing the Pillow

9. Cut fabric for pillow back to 20" x 11".

10. Refer to Technique 1 "How do I hook a simple design?" Steps 19–22 on page 29. Finish the pillow.

Tips

Hook a pillow with lettering in several different color ways and alternating the colors of the background and the lettering.

Make your pillow larger by adding onto the border around the outside of the pillow. Hook the border in the same color as the lettering.

How do I make a tote bag?

Because it is weighty, a hooked piece makes a perfect panel on a purse or tote bag. Simply size your design to the dimensions you would like for your tote.

Chicken Tote Bag (See photo on page 52)

The finished size of the tote bag is 15" x 12".
The hooked chicken measures 12" x 9".

HERE'S HOW:

Preparing the Backing

1. Using ruler and permanent marking pen, center and draw outside borderlines, 12" x 9", directly onto backing fabric.

2. Refer to "How do I transfer the pattern onto the backing fabric?" on page 19. Transfer Chicken Tote Bag Pattern on page 71 onto backing fabric, centered within outside borderline.

3. Refer to "How do I prepare the backing fabric for hooking?" on page 20. Machine-stitch around outside borderline and position backing fabric in frame.

Hooking the Design

4. Refer to "How do I cut the wool?" on page 18. Cut the wool into strips.

5. Refer to Technique 1 "How do I hook a simple design?" Steps 5–9 on pages 27–29. Hook chicken, following contour of wing and body to simulate direction feathers would lay.

WHAT YOU NEED TO GET STARTED

Materials:
Fabric for tote bag lining, 15" x 11" (2)
Felt for tote bag interlining, 15" x 12"
Monk's cloth for backing, 15" x 18"
Wool:
   black for tote bag, 1 yd.;
   gold for background, 1 yd.;
   red for comb and wattle, ¼ yd.;
   red plaid for border and chicken, 1½ yds.

Additional Supplies:
Velcro® or snap closure

6. Hook outside border.

7. Hook background area in small random forms until it is filled.

Preparing the Hooked Design for Finishing

8. Refer to "How do I steam a hooked design?" on page 22. Remove hooked design from frame, then steam hooked design.

Finishing the Tote Bag

9. Cut one 15" x 12" piece, two 2" x 12" strips, two 2" x 15" strips, and two 2" x 28" strips from black wool.

10. Place hooked design with one 2" x 12" wool strip on either side of hooked hen on work surface with right sides together and hooked side up. Machine-stitch along outside edge of first row of hooking. *Note: Stitching along the hooked line keeps your backing fabric from showing through when the piece is turned.*

11. Repeat Step 10 with 2" x 15" wool strips for top and bottom of hooked design.

12. Press seam allowance away from hooked piece, then trim seam allowance to reduce bulk.

13. Baste interlining to wrong side of 15" x 12" piece of black wool for tote back.

14. With right sides together, machine-stitch lining pieces along top edges of tote front and back pieces. Press seam allowance toward lining, then trim seam allowance.

15. With right sides together, machine-stitch tote and lining fronts and backs together, leaving a 5"–6" opening in the lining. Press and trim seam allowance.

16. Pull tote through opening in lining to turn right side out. Hand-stitch opening in lining closed.

17. With right sides together, fold over bottom edge corners matching seams and stitch across triangle approximately 1" from corner. Repeat on lining. *Note: This creates the boxed corners.*

18. Push lining down into tote and press top edge.

19. For each 2" x 28" strip of black wool, fold ½" in on both long edges and press. Fold over again and machine-stitch together, close to the edge. Repeat machine-stitch on the other side of folded strap.

20. Place approximately 1" of strap inside tote, 2" from side edges. Hand- or machine-stitch securely.

21. Following manufacturer's instructions, add snap or Velcro closure at inside center of purse.

CHICKEN TOTE BAG PATTERN   ENLARGE 140%

7 PROJECT

WHAT YOU NEED TO GET STARTED

Materials:

Burlap for backing, 23" x 18"

Fabric for pillow back, ½ yd.

Polyester stuffing

Wool:

assorted plaids for flowers, several strips;

black for checkerboard basket, 10" x 12";

bronze for checkerboard basket, 10" x 12";

gold for background, ¾ yd.;

green for flower stems, 12" square;

red for border and flowers, ¼ yd.

How do I hook a primitive floral design?

This sort of design is easy to "make it up" as you go. Hook simple lines for flowers and stems, then go back and fill in the background around them afterward.

Basket of Flowers Pillow (See photo on page 8)

The finished size of the pillow is: 17" x 12".

HERE'S HOW:

Preparing the Backing

1. Using ruler and permanent marking pen, center and draw outside borderlines, 17" x 12", directly onto backing fabric.

2. Refer to "How do I transfer the pattern onto the backing fabric?" on page 19. Transfer Basket of Flowers Pillow Pattern on page 74 onto backing fabric, centered within outside borderline.

3. Refer to "How do I prepare the backing fabric for hooking?" on page 20. Machine-stitch around outside borderline and position backing fabric in frame.

Hooking the Pillow

4. Refer to "How do I cut the wool?" on page 18. Cut the wool into strips.

5. Refer to Technique 1 "How do I hook a simple design?" Steps 5–9 on pages 27–29. Hook basket with checkerboard design. Hook flowers and stems.

6. Hook two rows for border.

7. Hook background area in small random forms until it is filled.

Preparing the Hooked Design for Finishing

8. Refer to "How do I steam a hooked design?" on page 22. Remove hooked design from frame, then steam hooked design.

Finishing the Pillow

9. Cut fabric for pillow back to 18" x 13".

10. Refer to Technique 1 "How do I hook a simple design?" Steps 19–22 on page 29. Finish the pillow.

How do I combine three design elements?

Successful designs are often worked up with three elements. These elements do not have to have common colors or shapes. This design uses three different colors and three different forms. As you can see, a black bird perched on a gold star with red lettering overhead works.

Liberty Crow Pillow (See photo on page 2)

The finished size of the pillow is 14" square.

HERE'S HOW:

Preparing the Backing

1. Using ruler and permanent marking pen, center and draw outside borderlines, 14" square, directly onto backing fabric.

2. Refer to "How do I transfer the pattern onto the backing fabric?" on page 19. Transfer Liberty Crow Pillow Pattern on page 86 onto backing fabric, centered within outside borderline.

3. Refer to "How do I prepare the backing fabric for hooking?" on page 20. Machine-stitch around outside borderline and position backing fabric in frame.

Hooking the Pillow

4. Refer to "How do I cut the wool?" on page 18. Cut the wool into strips.

5. Refer to Technique 1 "How do I hook a simple design?" Steps 5–9 on pages 27–29. Hook crow.

WHAT YOU NEED TO GET STARTED

Materials:
Fabric for pillow back, ½ yd.
Monk's cloth for backing, 20" square
Polyester stuffing
Wool:
  black for crow, ¼ yd.;
  blue for background, ½ yd.;
  dark red for border, lettering, and star outline, ½ yd.;
  gold for stars, ¼ yd.

Additional Supplies:
Buttons:
  large for large star (1);
  small for pillow corners (4)

6. Refer to Technique 2 "How do I hook a point and finish a round shape?" Steps 4–10 pages 30–31. Hook star.

7. Hook lettering and fill in around letters with background color.

8. Hook four corner stars.

9. Refer to Technique 5 "How do I hook a border and finish a rug?" Steps 7–8 on page 41. Begin hooking border of rug 1½" from outside border-line. Hook five rows around inner borderline.

10. Hook border color around stars.

11. Hook background area in small random forms until it is filled.

Preparing the Hooked Design for Finishing

12. Refer to "How do I steam a hooked design?" on page 22. Remove hooked design from frame, then steam hooked design.

Finishing the Pillow

13. Stitch large button onto center of large star. Stitch one small button onto center of small star at each corner.

14. Cut fabric for pillow back to 15" square.

15. Refer to Technique 1 "How do I hook a simple design?" Steps 19–22 on page 29. Finish the pillow.

LIBERTY CROW PILLOW PATTERN   ENLARGE 230%

Materials:

Monk's cloth for backing,
    23" x 27"
Rug binding tape, 1½" wide,
    3 yds.
Wool:
    black for roof and windows,
        ¼ yd.;
    gold for border, flowers,
        and lettering, ½ yd.;
    green for grass, ¼ yd.;
    moss green for flower stems
        and leaves, ¼ yd.;
    navy blue for background,
        1 yd.;
    red for house, ¼ yd.;
    red plaid for flowers, ¼ yd.;
    yellow for flower centers,
        10" x 12"
Wool yarn, gold, 1 skein

Additional Supplies:

#13 tapestry needle

How do I hook
a table mat?

Just about any design can be hooked for use as a table mat. Those with a home or floral theme are especially nice when presented on a kitchen or dining-room table.

Home Sweet Home Table Mat

The finished size of the table mat is 17" x 21".

HERE'S HOW:

Preparing the Backing

1. Using ruler and permanent marking pen, center and draw outside borderlines, 17" x 21", directly onto backing fabric.

2. Refer to "How do I transfer the pattern onto the backing fabric?" on page 19. Transfer Home Sweet Home Pattern on page 80 onto backing fabric, centered within outside borderline.

3. Refer to "How do I prepare the backing fabric for hooking?" on page 20. Machine-stitch around outside borderline and position backing fabric in frame.

Hooking the Table Mat

4. Refer to "How do I cut the wool?" on page 18. Cut the wool into strips.

5. Refer to Technique 1 "How do I hook a simple design?" Steps 5–9 on pages 27–29. Hook house outline. Hook windows and door, then hook inner area. Hook flowers. Hook lettering. *Note: Because the doors and window are "sitting on top" of your house pattern, you hook them first.*

6. Hook inside border with blue, 1" from outside borderline.

7. Hook background area in small random forms until it is filled.

8. Hook grass.

9. Refer to Technique 5 "How do I hook a border and finish a rug?" Steps 7–8 on page 41. Hook three rows with gold around inside border.

Preparing the Hooked Design for Finishing

10. Refer to "How do I steam a hooked design?" on page 22. Remove hooked design from frame, then steam hooked design.

Finishing the Table Mat

11. Refer to Technique 5 "How do I hook a border and finish a rug?" Steps 11–13 on page 42. Finish edges and back of table mat.

How do I hook a purse?

This charming purse started as a design for a pillow. However, its size and shape were perfect for something more utilitarian. There are many designs that can be converted into a purse.

Ladybug Purse (See photo on page 83)

The finished size of the purse is 8" x 10".

HERE'S HOW:

Preparing the Backing
1. Refer to "How do I transfer the pattern onto the backing fabric?" on page 19. Transfer Ladybug Purse Pattern on page 82 onto backing fabric.

2. Refer to "How do I prepare the backing fabric for hooking?" on page 20. Machine-stitch around outside borderline and position backing fabric in frame.

Hooking the Design
3. Refer to "How do I cut the wool?" on page 18. Cut the wool into strips.

4. Refer to Technique 1 "How do I hook a simple design?" Steps 5–9 on pages 27–29. Hook ladybug body and head.

5. Refer to Project 3 "How do I hook polka dots and embellishments? Step 9 on page 62. Hook dots.

Preparing the Hooked Design for Finishing
6. Refer to "How do I steam a hooked design?" on page 22. Remove hooked design from frame, then steam hooked design.

WHAT YOU NEED TO GET STARTED

Materials:
Monk's cloth for backing, 14" x 16"

Satin cord for purse handle, black, ¾ yd.

Wool:
black for back of purse and lining, ½ yd.

black for dots and head, ¼ yd.;

red for body, ¼ yd.;

Additional Supplies:
Snap closure, large, black

facing up. Machine-stitch along outside edge of first row of hooking only around body of ladybug.

11. Machine-stitch lining pieces together around body, leaving a 4" to 5" opening for turning.

12. Trim seam allowance to reduce bulk, then turn right side out through opening in lining.

13. Hand-stitch opening in lining closed. Push lining down into purse. Steam edges.

14. Following manufacturer's instructions, add snap at top of ladybug head to keep purse closed.

LADYBUG PURSE PATTERN
ENLARGE 270%

Finishing the Purse

7. Cut three 9" x 11" pieces from black wool, one for purse back and two for lining front and back.

8. Place ends of cord approximately ¼" from neck of ladybug. Hand- or machine-stitch securely.

9. With right sides together, machine-stitch one lining piece each to hooked design and purse back beginning 1" from "neck" and only around "head" of ladybug. Trim seams to reduce bulk. Flip "body" of each lining piece up over head.

10. Place hooked piece and purse back on work surface with right sides together and hooked side

How do I use several colors in a single motif?

WHAT YOU NEED TO GET STARTED

Materials:
Fabric for pillow back, ½ yd.
Monk's cloth for backing,
  20" x 18"
Polyester stuffing
Wool:
  black for base and cat, ¼ yd.;
  blue for flag and string,
    10" x 12";
  brown for background,
    ½ yd.;
  red for border, lettering,
    and wheels, ¼ yd.;
  white for cat body and flag,
    ¼ yd.

This simple cat pull toy is designed in two colors—black and white. It incorporates red and blue accents on the base of the toy and on the cat's flag-like tail. Placed against a solid background, all of the colors have equal importance.

Cat Pull Toy Pillow (See photo on page 53)

The finished size of the pillow is 14" x 12".

HERE'S HOW:

Preparing the Backing
1. Using ruler and permanent marking pen, center and draw outside borderlines, 14" x 12", directly onto backing fabric.

2. Refer to "How do I transfer the pattern onto the backing fabric?" on page 19. Transfer Cat Pull Toy Pillow Pattern on page 86 onto backing fabric, centered within outside borderline.

3. Refer to "How do I prepare the backing fabric for hooking?" on page 20. Machine-stitch around outside borderline and position backing fabric in frame.

Hooking the Pillow
4. Refer to "How do I cut the wool?" on page 18. Cut the wool into strips.

5. Refer to Technique 1 "How do I hook a simple design?" Steps 5–9 on pages 27–29. Hook cat with wheels first. Hook flag and base. Hook lettering and pull toy string.

6. Begin hooking border of rug ¾" from outside borderline. Hook two rows around inner borderline.

7. Hook background area in small random forms until it is filled.

Preparing the Hooked Design for Finishing

8. Refer to "How do I steam a hooked design?" on page 22. Remove hooked design from frame, then steam hooked design.

Finishing the Pillow

9. Cut fabric for pillow back to 15" x 13".

10. Refer to Technique 1 "How do I hook a simple design?" Steps 19–22 on page 29. Finish the pillow.

Tip

Try hooking this design with pastel colors for use in a traditional nursery. You could use gray in the place of the black, pink in the place of the red, and light blue in the place of the blue.

How do I hook a "play on words?"

The houses set within the body of the cat are a whimsical pictorial for the words "house cat." In your own designs, you can experiment with other such figures of speech.

House Cat Rug

The finished size of this rug is 29" x 24".

HERE'S HOW:

Tea-dyeing the Wool

1. Refer to Technique 6 "How do I tea-dye wool?" Steps 1–4 on page 44. Tea-dye white wool.

Preparing the Backing

2. Using ruler and permanent marking pen, center and draw outside borderlines, 29" x 24", directly onto backing fabric. Write "HOUSE CAT" along each side within border area.

3. Refer to "How do I transfer the pattern onto the backing fabric?" on page 19. Transfer House Cat Rug Pattern on page 89 onto backing fabric, centering cat within border.

4. Refer to "How do I prepare the backing fabric for hooking?" on page 20. Machine-stitch around outside borderline and position backing fabric in frame.

Hooking the Rug

5. Refer to "How do I cut the wool?" on page 18. Cut the wool into strips.

WHAT YOU NEED TO GET STARTED

Materials:
Monk's cloth for backing, 35" x 30"
Rug binding tape, 1½" wide, 4 yds.
Wool:
    black for eyes, houses, and whiskers, ¼ yd.;
    blue for background, lettering, and outside borderline of rug, 1½ yds.;
    red for border and houses, 1½ yds.;
    white for cat, ⅓ yd.;
    yellow for house, 10" x 12"
Wool yarn, blue, 1½ skeins

Additional Supplies:
3 oz. jar of instant tea
#13 tapestry needle
White vinegar

6. Refer to Technique 1 "How do I hook a simple design?" Steps 5–9 on pages 27–29. Hook outline of cat first. Hook houses inside cat. Hook eyes, whiskers, mouth, and nose. Hook inner area of cat.

7. Refer to Technique 5 "How do I hook a border and finish a rug?" Steps 7–8 on page 41. Begin hooking inside border 3¼" from outside borderline. Hook two rows with red.

8. Hook lettering with blue and fill in around letters with red. Continue hooking border area until it is filled.

9. Hook outside border with blue.

10. Hook background area in small random forms until it is filled.

Preparing the Hooked Design for Finishing

11. Refer to "How do I steam a hooked design?" on page 22. Remove hooked design from frame, then steam hooked design.

Finishing the Rug

12. Refer to Technique 5 "How do I hook a border and finish a rug?" Steps 11–13 on page 42. Finish edges and back of rug.

HOUSE CAT RUG PATTERN   ENLARGE 275%

Materials:
Monk's cloth for backing,
  16" square
Polyester stuffing
Wool:
  black for eyes, 12" square;
  cream for face, ½ yd.;
  plaid for hair and pillow
    back, ½ yd.;
  red for cheeks, mouth, and
    nose, ¼ yd.

How do I make a face pillow with shaggy hair?

The extra-wide wool strips sewn into the seam of the finished pillow complete the rag doll's face and add texture to the piece.

Rag Doll's Face Pillow (See photo on page 7)

The finished size of this pillow is 10" in diameter.

HERE'S HOW:

Preparing the Backing

1. Using ruler and permanent marking pen, center and draw a 10" circle directly onto backing fabric.

2. Refer to "How do I transfer the pattern onto the backing fabric?" on page 19. Transfer Rag Doll's Face Pattern on opposite page onto backing fabric, centered within outside borderline.

3. Refer to "How do I prepare the backing fabric for hooking?" on page 20. Machine-stitch around outside borderline and position backing fabric in frame.

Hooking the Pillow

4. Refer to "How do I cut the wool?" on page 18. Cut the wool into strips.

5. Refer to Technique 1 "How do I hook a simple design?" Steps 5–9 on pages 27–29. Hook nose first. Next, hook eyes and mouth. Finally, hook cheeks.

6. Hook borderline of pillow.

strips in half and placing them between the pillow back and the hooked piece with the folds positioned along the edge of the hairline. Turn pillow right side out so hair strips are sticking up between pillow back and front.

12. Tie each strip in a knot at edge of hooking.

Tip

You can make this pillow larger if you like. Simply increase the diameter of the pillow.

7. Hook background area in small random forms until it is filled.

RAG DOLL'S FACE PATTERN
ENLARGE 250%

Preparing the Hooked Design for Finishing

8. Refer to "How do I steam a hooked design?" on page 22. Remove hooked design from frame, then steam the hooked design.

Finishing the Pillow

9. Tear eight 1½" wide x 10" long strips of plaid wool for hair.

10. Cut fabric for the pillow back to 11" diameter.

11. Refer to Technique 1 "How do I hook a simple design?" Steps 19–22 on page 29. Finish the pillow, folding the hair

How do I use motifs on corners within a border?

Materials:
Monk's cloth for backing,
   31" x 25"
Rug binding tape, 1½" wide,
   3 yds.
Wool:
   black for eyes and lashes,
      ¼ yd.;
   navy blue for border,
      1 yd.;
   plaid for hair, ¼ yd.;
   red for face detail and
      lettering, ½ yd.;
   rose for cheeks, ¼ yd.;
   white for faces, ½ yd.;
   yellow for background
      around lettering, 1 yd.
Wool yarn, navy blue, 1 skein

Additional Supplies:
#13 tapestry needle

The border of this design fills in around the rag dolls' faces at each corner. This rug can be made larger if you like by spacing the faces further apart and filling in the area with border.

Old Rag Doll Rug

The finished size of this rug is 25" x 19".

HERE'S HOW:

Preparing the Backing
1. Using ruler and permanent marking pen, center and draw outside borderlines, 25" x 19", directly onto backing fabric.

2. Refer to "How do I transfer the pattern onto the backing fabric?" on page 19. Transfer Old Rag Doll Rug Pattern on page 94 onto backing fabric, centered within outside borderline.

3. Refer to "How do I prepare the backing fabric for hooking?" on page 20. Machine-stitch around outside borderline and position backing fabric in frame.

Hooking the Rug
4. Refer to "How do I cut the wool?" on page 18. Cut the wool into strips.

5. Refer to Technique 1 "How do I hook a simple design?" Steps 5–9 on pages 27–29. Hook outside borderline first, then hook inside borderline.

6. Hook lettering. Hook background around lettering and continue until completely filled in.

7. Hook nose, lips, eyes, and cheeks on faces first. Hook outline, then hook inner area of each face around features and continue until completely filled in.

8. Hook rows between borderlines until border is filled in.

9. Cut 48 strips of plaid wool, ½" wide and 5" long, for hair.

10. For hair on each face, push hook through backing fabric at top of head and pull up strip so end

is at front of hooking. Push hook one stitch over, just beside that end, and pull up remaining end of wool. Tie ends in a knot. Repeat until there are 12 strips on each face. Trim strips to desired length.

Preparing the Hooked Design for Finishing

11. Refer to "How do I steam a hooked design?" on page 22. Remove hooked design from frame, then steam hooked design.

Finishing the Rug

12. Refer to Technique 5 "How do I hook a border and finish a rug?" Steps 11–13 on page 42. Finish edges and back of rug.

Old Rag Doll Rug Pattern
Enlarge 280%

How do I hook a cover for a footstool?

You can hook a cover for any size stool you want. Measure the footstool top and add enough extra to cover the sides of the top.

Star Footstool Cover (See photo on page 3)

The finished size of this footstool cover is 12" x 9".

HERE'S HOW:

Preparing the Backing

1. Place footstool upside down on backing fabric and, using permanent marking pen, trace around shape of stool top.

2. Measure sides of stool edge, then add this dimension plus 1½" to entire size of stool top. Based on these measurements, draw outside borderline around shape of stool top. Draw inside border 1" from shape of stool top. *Note: When you place the hooked design on the stool, it will wrap around the sides and have enough left to tack on the underside of the stool.*

3. Refer to "How do I transfer the pattern onto the backing fabric?" on page 19. Trace Star Footstool Cover Pattern on page 96 onto backing fabric, centered within inside border.

4. Refer to "How do I prepare the backing fabric for hooking?" on page 20. Machine-stitch around outside borderline and position backing fabric in frame.

Hooking the Footstool Cover

5. Refer to "How do I cut the wool?" on page 18. Cut the wool into strips.

WHAT YOU NEED TO GET STARTED

Materials:

Materials:
Monk's cloth for backing, size of stool top plus 6" on each side
Wool:
gold for inside border and star, ¼ yd.;
red for background, diameter of stool top times five
Wool yarn, red, 1 yd.

Additional Supplies:

#13 tapestry needle
Hammer
Upholstery tacks (2 boxes)
Wooden footstool, oval-shaped

12. Gently pull the yarn ends to slightly gather the backing fabric.

13. Fit hooked design onto top of stool and pull yarn tighter until cover is on snugly. Tie off the yarn.

14. Turn stool upside down. Turn excess backing fabric under and tack with upholstery tacks all around edge of stool top to give it a finished look.

6. Refer to Technique 2 "How do I hook a point and finish a round shape?" Steps 4–10 on pages 30–31. Hook star.

7. Hook outside borderline.

8. Hook inside border.

9. Hook background area in small random forms until it is filled.

Preparing the Hooked Design for Finishing

10. Refer to "How do I steam a hooked design?" on page 22. Remove hooked design from frame, then steam hooked design.

Finishing the Cover

11. Thread tapestry needle with two strands of yarn. Make a running stitch around the edge of the design in backing fabric as close to the hooking as possible.

STAR FOOTSTOOL COVER PATTERN
ENLARGE 130%

How do I hook an odd-shaped rug?

16

PROJECT

For this rug, I copied the shape of a purchased mat that was designed to sit at the base of the kitchen sink. It was the perfect format for this front-door greeting.

Welcome Rug

The finished size of this rug is 38" x 24".

HERE'S HOW:

Preparing the Backing

1. Refer to "How do I transfer the pattern onto the backing fabric?" on page 19. Trace Welcome Rug Pattern on page 99 onto backing fabric.

2. Refer to "How do I prepare the backing fabric for hooking?" on page 20. Machine-stitch around outside borderline and position backing fabric in frame.

Hooking the Rug

3. Refer to "How do I cut the wool?" on page 18. Cut the wool into strips.

4. Refer to Technique 2 "How do I hook a point and finish a round shape?" Steps 4–10 on pages 30–31. Hook outline and inner area of three top stars first.

5. Refer to Technique 4 "How do I hook letters?" Steps 4–5 on page 36. Hook outline of lettering first, then hook inner areas.

6. Hook outline and inner area of five bottom stars.

WHAT YOU NEED TO GET STARTED

Materials:
Monk's cloth for backing, 44" x 30"
Rug binding tape, 1½" wide, 3¼ yds.
Wool:
   gold for inside border and stars, 1 yd.;
   khaki green for background, 2½ yds.;
   red for border and lettering, ¾ yd.
Wool yarn, red, 1 skein

Additional Supplies:
#13 tapestry needle

7. Refer to Technique 5 "How do I hook a border and finish a rug?" Steps 7–8 on page 41. Hook inside border with gold, 1½" from outside borderline. Hook five rows with red around the inside border.

8. Hook background area in small random forms until it is filled.

Preparing the Hooked Design for Finishing

9. Refer to "How do I steam a hooked design?" on page 22. Remove hooked design from frame, then steam the hooked design.

Finishing the Rug

10. Refer to Technique 5 "How do I hook a border and finish a rug?" Steps 11–13 on page 42. Finish edges and back of rug.

WELCOME RUG PATTERN
ENLARGE 430%

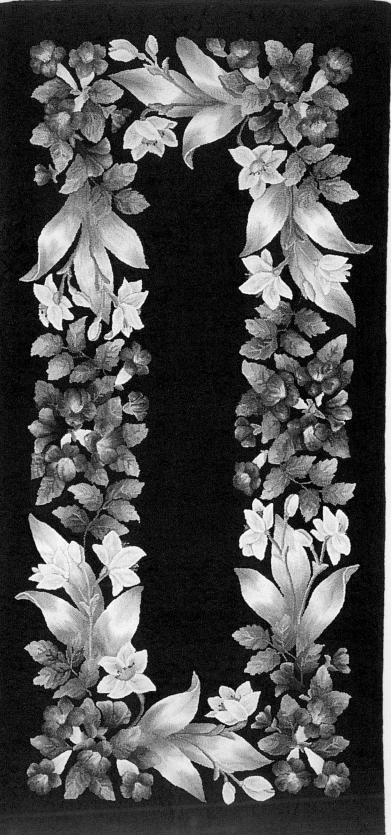

Section 4: the gallery

Karen Kahle

Karen Kahle refers to herself as a "wool painter." She has always loved fiber arts and has enjoyed quilting, batik, embroidery and silk painting. She has devoted the last four years to rug hooking and starting her own pattern business, Primitive Spirit, which currently offers 37 beautiful designs.

Beyond her patterns, she enjoys bringing new inspiration to the world of rug hooking. Karen developed a dye-less dyeing technique she calls "marbleized wool" that makes gorgeous colorful wool—a breakthrough for those who want lovely colors without dealing with dyes.

An avid herb gardener, her favorite subject has been flowers. Many of her designs are born from a love for nature and old-fashioned things. Color is her inspiration and her guiding force as she incorporates the unabashed spontaneity of the primitive rug hookers of the past into her own work.

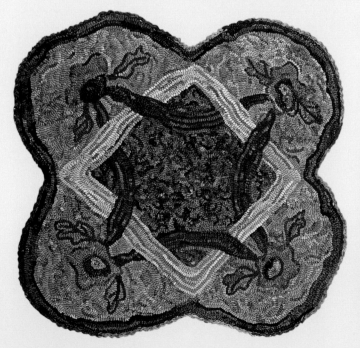

"Knot Garden"
designed and hooked by Karen Kahle
29" cloverleaf

"A Secret Garden"
designed and hooked by Karen Kahle
31" x 32"

"The Hermitage"
designed and hooked by Karen Kahle
26" x 32"

"A Towne Garden"
designed and hooked by Karen Kahle
31" x 32"

"Monticello"
designed and hooked
by Karen Kahle
40" x 31"

"Water Nymph"
designed by Jane McGown Flynn and hooked by Nancy Miller

Nancy Miller

Nancy Miller carries on the family tradition of rug hooking that began with her great grandmother.

A member of the Association of Traditional Hooking Artists and the McGown National Guild, she is also an accredited McGown teacher. Her work has won blue ribbons at the California State Fair every year since 1989 and has been featured in many books, magazines, and newsletters. She has participated in numerous workshops, trade shows, and exhibits throughout the United States.

Nancy hand-forges the Miller Hook and teaches classes at her studio. She owns and operates Miller Rug Hooking, a mail-order company specializing in quality hooks and hand-dyed rug-hooking kits.

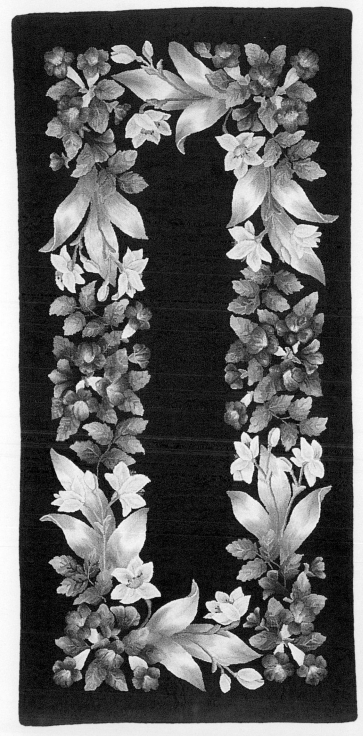

"Pansies"
designed by Jane McGown Flynn
and hooked by Nancy Miller

"Maple Leaves"
designed and hooked by Nancy Miller

"Lorna"
designed by Jane McGown Flynn
and hooked by Nancy Miller

"Grandma's Rug"
designed and hooked
by Nancy Miller

*This design is an
adaptation of Nancy's
grandmother's
(Florence Dean)
hooked rug from
the 1930s.*

"Cabin Repeat"
designed by
Jane McGown Flynn and
hooked by Nancy Miller

*This rug is hooked with
overdyed plaids and tweeds.*

About the Author

When I am not busily hooking rugs in my Napa Valley, California, home, I enjoy spending time with my husband John, a Captain with the District Attorney's office in Oakland, California. We have five boys and ten grandchildren.

I worked for a home accessory company in Dallas, Texas, for 23½ years. After retiring 10 years ago, I saw a picture in a magazine of a hooked footstool and, wanting to know more about hooking, I called the magazine. They put me in touch with Nancy Miller in Sacramento, California, a well-known instructor on hooking, whose work is featured in this book. I have been "hooked" on rug hooking for five years.

Since the time of my childhood, I have enjoyed creating. I wanted to be a fashion designer and, even as a child, I designed and created my own doll clothes. Designing rug-hooking patterns is a very satisfying way to challenge my creative energies.

Last year I started a pattern company, called "Woolsworth." I have a web site and sell my pattern packets to people all over the world.

It is my hope that when you read *Rug Hooking for the first time*® you will become hooked on rug hooking as well.

Donna

Dedication

This book is dedicated to my husband John for putting up with the little bits of wool I leave all over the place. With his love, support, and belief in me, this book became possible.

Special thanks to Donna Kooler at Kooler Design Studio for having faith in me and recommending me for this project.

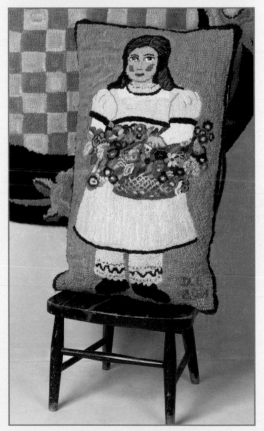

"Flower Girl"
designed and hooked
by Donna Lovelady
18" x 24"

*The Americana Santa and
the Stove Pipe Primitive Santa were
selected and featured in a prestigious
2002 publication devoted solely to the
subject of Santa Claus.*

"Americana Santa"
designed and hooked
by Donna Lovelady
18" x 4'

"Stove Pipe Primitive Santa"
designed and hooked
by Donna Lovelady
18" x 5'

"Sit-down Santa"
designed and hooked
by Donna Lovelady
12" x 18" sitting

"Labour of
Love"
designed and
hooked
by Donna Lovelady

*This 3' x 5' rug was
my first experience
with the craft of rug
hooking. I designed
it to go with a wall-
paper pattern in my
kitchen. It took nine
months to complete.*

Acknowledgments

Miller Rug Hooking
Nancy Miller
2448 Brentwood Road
Sacramento, CA 95825
1-916-482-1234
e-mail: millerrugs@aol.com

Miller Rug Hooking sells great wools, hooks, preprinted kits, and supplies.

The Dorr Mill Store
P.O. Box 88
Guild, NH 03754
1-800-846-DORR
e-mail: dorrmillstore@sugar-river.net
www.dorrmillstore.com

The Dorr Mill Store is a wonderful source of wools and backing materials.

W. Cushing & Company
21 North Street
P.O. Box 351
Kennebunkport, ME 04046
1-800-626-7847
e-mail: customer@wcushing.com
www.wcushing.com

W. Cushing & Company offers kits, tools, backing materials, books, as well as commercial dyes.

Tom Duffy
Duffy Lap Frame
1-315-393-8553
e-mail: tomduffy2@aol.com
www.northnet.org/tduffy

Tom Duffy supplied the hooking frame used by the author.

Gruber's
P.O. Box 87
Pierz, MN 56364
1-320-468-6553
www.grubersquiltshop.com

This is the home of the Gruber Hooking Frame.

I.W. Designs
800l Westmoreland Avenue
Pittsburgh, PA 15218
1-412-244-1844
e-mail: pghframe@aol.com
www.i-w-designs.com

I.W. Designs sells the Portable Lap Hooking Frame.

Harry M. Fraser Co.
433 Duggins Road
Stoneville, NC 27048
1-336-573-9830
e-mail: fraserrugs@aol.com
www.fraserrugs.com

Harry M. Fraser Co. manufactures mechanical wool cutters: Bliss model A, and Fraser 500-1.

Rigby
P.O. Box 158, Dept. RH
Bridgton, ME 04009

Rigby produces mechanical wool cutters.

Woolsworth
1000 Capitola Drive
Napa, CA 94559
1-707-224-4034
www.woolsworth.net

Woolsworth offers pattern packets for rug hooking and wool appliqué.

Sulky of America
3113 Broadpoint Drive
Harbor Heights, FL 33983

Sulky of America is the maker of the Sulky Iron-on Transfer Pen.

Hooked on Rugs
982 West Harper Road
Mason, MI 48854
1-517-244-9199

This shop carries the author's kits.

Books for Your Library

American Primitive Hooked Rugs,
Barbara Carroll & Emma Lou Lais
Wildwood Press
Kennebunkport, MA

Antique Colours for Primitive Rugs,
Barbara Carroll & Emma Lou Lais
W. Cushing & Co.

The Art of Rug Hooking, Anne D. Mather
Sterling Publishing Co., Inc. New York

Beautiful Wool, Laurice Heath
Cabin Ridge Press

Colors to Dye For,
Cynthia Gallant-Simpson
Hesperus Folk Art Gallery
1063 Main Street
P.O. Box 1771
Brewster, Cape Cod, MA 02631

Creative Rug Hooking, Anne D. Mather
Sterling Publishing Co., Inc. New York

The following publications are full of ideas and information. Each contains an advertising section that directs you to sources for ordering equipment and preprinted designs on backing fabrics. There are also numerous sources for wool if you do not want to use recycled wool. Each magazine publishes five issues per year.

Rug Hooking Magazine
1300 Market Street Ste. 202
Lemoyne, PA 17043-9943
1-800-233-9055

Association of Traditional Hooking Artists (ATHA)
Membership Chairman
1360 Newman Avenue
Seekonk, MA 02771
1-508-399-8230

If you become a member of ATHA, you can borrow from their free lending library. Their library contains a variety of books on rug hooking as well as back issues of both magazines.

Metric Equivalency Chart

inches to millimetres and centimetres (mm-millimetres cm-centimetres)

inches	mm	cm	inches	cm	inches	cm	inches	cm
⅛	3	0.3	6	15.2	21	53.3	36	91.4
¼	6	0.6	7	17.8	22	55.9	37	94.0
⅜	10	1.0	8	20.3	23	58.4	38	96.5
½	13	1.3	9	22.9	24	61.0	39	99.1
⅝	16	1.6	10	25.4	25	63.5	40	101.6
¾	19	1.9	11	27.9	26	66.0	41	104.1
⅞	22	2.2	12	30.5	27	68.6	42	106.7
1	25	2.5	13	33.0	28	71.1	43	109.2
1¼	32	3.2	14	35.6	29	73.7	44	111.8
1½	38	3.8	15	38.1	30	76.2	45	114.3
1¾	44	4.4	16	40.6	31	78.7	46	116.8
2	51	5.1	17	43.2	32	81.3	47	119.4
3	76	7.6	18	45.7	33	83.8	48	121.9
4	102	10.2	19	48.3	34	86.4	49	124.5
5	127	12.7	20	50.8	35	88.9	50	127.0

Index